From A Father's Perspective (On His Own)

JOHNATHAN E. MCFADDEN

From A Father's Perspective (On His Own)

Copyright © 2021 by *Johnathan E. McFadden*

All rights reserved. No part of this publication may be reproduced, distributed, or transmitted in any form or by any means, including photocopying, recording, or other electronic or mechanical methods, without the prior written permission of the author, except in the case of brief quotations embodied in critical reviews and certain other non-commercial uses permitted by copyright law.

ISBN
978-1-956529-36-4 (Paperback)
978-1-956529-35-7 (eBook)

CONTENTS

From A Father's Perspective On His Own 1

You Can Cry For a Day 7

Moving On Up 11

Understanding the Process 15

Overcoming Adversity 21

Don't Believe the Hype 33

Thy Will Was Done 49

The Man behind the Perspective 71

Where Are They Now 85

FROM A FATHER'S PERSPECTIVE ON HIS OWN

In June of 2005, my son Jaevery McFadden left home from Riviera Beach, Florida to go to the Midwest. Jaevery received a full football scholarship to a Big Ten University and was arriving for summer conditioning. I would talk with him nightly about his daily activities like, "how was the running?" "how was the weightlifting?" His answer would always be, "it's going good daddy". Days went by with the same type of correspondence. I would also look on the websites of his university just to keep up with what was going on.

While checking the website one day, I saw where a freshman running back was arrested. Taken in for questioning were Jaevery McFadden and three more of his friends. I'm thinking this must have just happened because I just talked to Jaevery last night and he never mentioned anything to me. When I looked at the date, the incident happened three days prior. I immediately called Jaevery to find out what happened and why wasn't I informed when the incident happened. Jaevery explained how some young men from the area were attempting to jump his friend the freshman running back and they did what they needed to do to make sure that didn't happen. Doing what they needed to do mean that they fought those young men from Madison. The reason he gave me for not letting me know immediately was that he was only questioned and not arrested. He felt like it was no big deal. We talked about things like that were something me and his mother needed to know immediately. I told him that I didn't want the internet to be the place where I found out this type of information about my son. He assured me that it wouldn't happen again. Thanks be to God it never did.

As fall camp rolled around we would have the same types of conversations concerning his progress and understanding of his position which was tight end at the time. During the actual practices Jaevery did a lot of standing around and he worked with the scout team. The scout team is the young men that perform what plays that the opposing team will be trying to execute on game day. Jaevery and his scout team teammates' job were to give the number one and the number two offense and defense the best possible look that they could. We talked about allowing this time to be a time to learn. We talked about getting use to the speed of the game and making plays while he is on the field. I would tell him now he had a chance to evaluate himself when he saw himself on film. I told him if you can make plays against the number ones and twos you can play against Ohio State and Michigan.

It was decided by the coaches that Jaevery would redshirt. Redshirt is when a player is allowed to miss a year of competition but, is allowed to be involved in all the other team functions. This usually happens when the younger player is behind older players that have experience and have been contributors in the previous years. Injuries also played a big part. Jaevery and I felt this was advantageous for him because there was three fifth year seniors in front of him lead by a young man with a lot of talent, who played with The Houston Texans, Baltimore Ravens and is now playing with The Denver Broncos.

Classes started and our conversation expanded to academics. We talked about using the tutors and study hall not only as an option, but as an advantage. I would often mention to Jaevery that he was in a diamond mine and he has the opportunity to pick and shape his diamond the way that he wanted. I would also reiterate how I wish I would have taken advantage of my opportunity to go to the University of Michigan. I would talk about how Coach Bo Schembechler came and recruited me.

We were at my senior year football banquet at a restaurant called the Sweden House. I had just received the best defensive back trophy. I gave the trophy to my mother and went to the ice cream machine. I had a cone in my hand and felt someone tap me on my right shoulder. I turned around and it was coach Schembechler. He asked me if I was interested in a football scholarship to the University of Michigan. I stated that I was being recruited in basketball, which I loved. He told me to get in touch with a man by the name of Mr. Dan Calloway in two weeks. I grew up playing all sports in the Riviera Beach Recreation Department where Mr. Calloway was the director. Mr. Calloway had mitigated the scholarship for my friend Anthony A.C. Carter the year before. A.C. was a first team All-American his sophomore year and was tenth in the Heisman Trophy that year also. He would eventually end up a three time All-American wide receiver and placing seventh and fourth in the Heisman Trophy his junior and senior years respectively. I had just as much talent as A.C. I was an All-State defensive back. That opportunity passed me by. Who dropped the ball I don't know. My mother and my father knew nothing about recruiting and neither did any of my older brothers or sisters. I'm the seventh out of nine children. I had no uncle or family friend to make sure that opportunity wasn't missed. So, I would often remind Jaevery that he was blessed to be where he was. But, I learn so much from that experience. By what was not provided for me at the time, I made sure that I would be the provider of it for Jaevery.

As the 2005 season got under way, the University that Jaevery attended was on television a lot. I would scan the sidelines when the camera was on Jaevery team to see if I could find Jaevery. When I did I would yell to my wife "there's Jae"!!! Jae is what my wife, family and friends called Jaevery. These games I would also record. I would put the times that the VCR showed down on paper so that I could go back and look at when Jaevery was spotted. The elation I felt when I saw Jaevery on that television went beyond proud. I was watching a young man who told his father that he wanted to play college football fulfill one of his dreams.

Fall passed and winter approached with the team Jaevery played for playing an exciting brand of football. They were very opportunistic on defense and had a clock controlling offense. My wife and I had long decided that we were coming to Family Day. Family Day is the game where the seniors would be introduced to the fans and they would run and meet their family at the forty five yard line. It was a rainy and cold November Saturday night. My wife and I brought big jackets for this occasion but, we left them in the car we rented. We were thinking that the rain would subside but, it didn't. It stayed rainy and cold throughout the game. We sat closer together as each seniors name was called. As I watched the family pride, joy and jubilation on the faces of everyone, I made a deal with God. I asked him if HE would allow me to see this happen with my son that I would get on my knees with my hands raised high in front of these 84,000 people. The university that Jaevery played for would go on to lose to the Iowa Hawkeyes. The university that Jaevery played foe continued to play well throughout the month of November and went on to receive a birth in the Capital One bowl against the Auburn Tigers. Jaevery and I talked about using this extra practice time to show the coaches what he could do. The coaches would use a good amount of practice time as developmental time for the underclassmen. I would emphasize to Jaevery not to waste any reps. We talked about learning from every aspect of what he was going through. The bowl game experience was a good reward for me and rest of the family also, with the game being play in Orlando, Florida. The drive is only two and a half hours from Riviera Beach. The university that Jaevery played for would go on to defeat Auburn and finish the season 9-4. Jaevery would return home with me and my wife. He was given a package with plays and a workout regimen. When I got off from work, he and I would head to the park and put in work. I would throw him one hundred to one hundred and fifty balls, we would run all the routes that a tight end could run. We worked on depth, getting in and out of his breaks quick and looking the ball into his hands. Jaevery got good work with me throwing him the ball because my arm is still NFL caliber right now. In the Florida winter of 2006 it was just as good. Catching the football was not going to be a reason that Jaevery wouldn't be on the field playing tight end that spring and upcoming season. Jaevery could catch a bee bee in the dark.

YOU CAN CRY FOR A DAY

Jaevery would report to winter conditioning and do all his workouts with his position group, the tight ends. The three fifth year seniors are gone and the competition for the starting tight end and backup tight end positions were up in the air. Jaevery, another redshirt freshman tight end and a senior were the leading candidates to fill those rolls. The conversations after we talked about the strength and conditioning would move to "how are your classes coming"? His answer would always be, dad everything is okay. I stop calling every night, calling myself letting him have his freedom. I was probably calling two to three times a week. Spring practice 2006 started with Jaevery not getting the number of reps you would think someone who was second on the depth chart would get. Practice after practice the same thing, maybe a play or three at the end of practice. This went on for about another three day then I get a call from a crying son saying "daddy, they moved me to Sam linebacker". The Sam linebacker is the linebacker that usually line up on the side where the tight end is or the strong side of the offense which is the side that have the most receivers. Jaevery talked about how he wasn't even in the plans at the tight end position. He was heartbroken after working so hard and not being given an opportunity to fail or succeed. In high school Jaevery's team ran plays behind him when he played tight end, so I knew he could block. On his high school film the coaches saw how he took on fullbacks and defensive linemen so that couldn't be the problem. Catching the ball couldn't be the problem because he wasn't thrown the ball enough during the practices to make a judgment. It was just, you are a linebacker now, deal with it. I told Jaevery that "you could cry for a day". I went on to tell Jaevery that he was only given a lemon and now it was time to make lemonade. I prayed on the phone with Jaevery asking God to give Jaevery the necessary peace he would need to be successful in that transition. I also told him to read Psalm 119:97-100. This passage of scripture talks about how you can be wiser than your teacher. I told him to make that his anthem.

Personally, the move was kind of strange. You recruit a kid at a position and he have to go 1500 miles to find out that playing tight end for the university that he played at wasn't going to happen. The coach that recruited Jaevery would move from the defensive coordinator to the head coach. His conversation with me stopped Jaevery and me from taking a visit to the University of Illinois where my niece was on scholarship running track. Coach Ron Zook sat in my living room and gave a great sales pitch but, we had respect for coach that recruited Jaevery. I can still remember the conversation we had. I ask the coach that recruited Jaevery what was the problem with Jaevery taking the visit to Illinois? The coach stated that Jaevery was already committed to their university. Then he said to me that you and Bev, my wife, are married right, would she allow you to go and see another woman? With that being said we didn't take the visit to Illinois. Loyalty is only a word with coaches; they don't practice what they preach. Jaevery was a first team all-state utility player in class five A football here in Florida. Five A football is just as good or better than six A football was during and after Jaevery's high school career. Jaevery was good enough to recruit, but not good enough to play. During this time I found myself being a pastor, psychiatrist, therapist, educator, philosopher and last but not least a father to Jaevery.

I arrived in that Midwest City to watch spring practice. Before practice started, I visited the head coach in his office. My intention was just to say hi, how are you doing? , what's up? I wasn't there to vent or find out why Jaevery's position was changed. We spoke then the head coach talked about how Jaevery was about a year or two from being able to help the team. I listened and we talked about how the family was doing and I shook his and left. I never believed in trying to tell a coach how to run his team. I'm from the old school where prayer changes things. I attended about eight practices. There were several people ahead of Jaevery on the depth chart at the linebacker position. Throughout the time Jaevery was in that Midwest City, I was always praying for him. I would ask God to move on Jaevery's behalf concerning academics, football, girls, and just all aspects of his life. As the spring game approached, Jaevery would be upset about not getting reps and making mistakes when he did get reps. In the spring game I think he played about the last five plays of the game where he did make a couple of tackles.

My main reason for watching spring practices and the spring game was to see the talent level. I've been a world class athlete all my life. One of the best things I do is assessing talent. I watched the two tight ends that they allowed to play and the only difference was that they were given the opportunity. They were also coached differently. When they made a mistake they weren't yelled at, they were talked to. I also wanted to see if these linebackers were actually better than Jaevery so I could tell him he needed to step his game up. My assessment ended with Jaevery being told that not playing right now is the coach's preference. I also told Jaevery that I didn't see a linebacker that was better than him. We talked about continuing to be a good teammate, friend and player and things would change. We also talk about his anthem Psalms 119:97-100. We talked about meditating on that scripture and making it apart of his daily regimen.

MOVING ON UP

With spring practice and the game now over, the conversations now consist of strength and conditioning, study hall and tutoring, girls and my ticket to come home. When Jaevery did come home we would work on the linebacker drills concerning depth in the passing game, hook and curl drops and covering the seams. I had a room in the house with about four hundred pounds of weights and we'd lift. Jaevery being home gave us time to interface as father and son as well as son to father. I would always tell him that the head coach didn't control his destiny and that God does. We would talk about the defensive coordinators not being able to control his destiny and that God does. I would often just grab his hand and say let's pray. Jaevery was always receptive to me doing this. This goes back to when Jaevery was born. Jaevery use to fall asleep on my chest from birth to about eighteen months old. God allowed me to feel Jaevery's need and love for me. That became very evident one day when Jaevery and I visited my brother and his two sons at his home. Jaevery was playing with his two cousins about thirty feet away from where my brother and I was watching T.V. Jaevery walked over to me and it was apparent that he was having trouble breathing. My brother begins pounding Jaevery in the back and nothing came out of his mouth. My brother continued to pound and nothing came out of Jaevery's mouth. I then quickly reached in his mouth swooped my finger in the back of his throat and a piece of plastic candy paper was on my finger. Jaevery cried a little then went back playing with his cousins. What makes an eighteen month old boy know that he is in trouble and to walk pass his uncle, who was closer to him, come to his father for help. God is good isn't HE? About a week before this incident my job sent me to a First Aid &CPR class. I was told that you can just go there and sign up and they would send your card to your job. Something inside told me to go to that training. When I got there the small room was packed and you could barely see the facilitator from the back. Again, I could have signed my name and left without any reprocautions. I went to the front where I learned the necessary maneuvers to save Jaevery's life. If I didn't go to that training and make my way to the front, I wouldn't be writing this book. The Holy Spirit was on me to get this training because HE knew that I would need it later.

Jaevery left in June of 2006 for summer classes and strength and conditioning. Now I was calling once or twice a week, again, calling myself given him his freedom. My wife would ask me if I talked to Jae today and I would say no. My wife was having a hard time understanding how Jaevery was going to reach the goals he set for himself if he was not being given an opportunity. I would always tell her "The head coach do not control Jaevery's life and that God does". Her heart really hurt seeing Jaevery go through that adverse time. She talked about how all his friends he came in with were becoming starters and he was being left behind.

Strength and conditioning along with classes were going well. Fall camp 2006 begins with Jaevery third on the depth chart at strong side linebacker. I was always checking the websites to see what the coaches were saying about the way practices were going and who was being impressive. Jaevery would tell me that he was coming along and getting more familiar with the terminology of the defense each practice. I wanted to hear it from the coaches so I would check the websites to read what was being said. There were some injuries to starting linebackers. This would allow Jaevery to work at both outside linebacker positions. I can recall an article where the defensive coordinator was ask the question, which young player made the most out of the opportunity with the three starters being out hurt. The defensive coordinatior talked about how Jaevery had a good understanding of what was going on and how well he had picked things up. He also talked about Jaevery's quickness, aggressiveness and how he wanted to be good. He stated, although Jaevery was still making mistakes, he liked the way that Jaevery was coming along. The work that Jaevery got was with the first team defense. Injuries to other players had thrusted him behind both starters. When the starters would return, Jaevery was move up to second team behind the starting weak side linebacker.

I arrived in that Midwest City to watch and critique Jaevery on his progress. He would look good on some plays then not as good on others. Overall you could tell he belonged. Jaevery's mistakes came with some choice curse word from the head coach and the defensive coordinator. When the starters would make a mistake all you would here was "run it again". The choice curse words were reserved for certain people. As a former player and coach, I could understand the approach. But, your team will be much better if you, as a coach, could openly criticize your best players in front of the team. That way when players that you deemed who you can embarrass and demean anytime you got ready want feel as bad because they see that you handle everyone the same. Jaevery and I would talk about not letting what the coaches were saying effect his focus. Two practices a day some days and meetings until 10:30pm at night can be and usually is draining. When I would talk to Jaevery at about 11:15pm central time and 12:15am eastern, I could feel he needed to hear a word of encouragement. I would always tell him how proud I was of him and that I loved him. Sometimes he would reply back, thanks daddy I needed that. Another quote that I would leave him with before I hung up the phone was, "tell the Lord thank you".

UNDERSTANDING THE PROCESS

If you are going to be great at anything it usually takes dedication, commitment and preparation. There is always a process that you have to go through. When you are able to grasp and understand the process, it makes everything that much easier. It's like taking a test. When you have studied for two weeks on the subject matter, when you see the test it is easy. You say bring it on. But, if you are not familiar with the subject matter and you receive the test, fear and apprehension set in and you don't do well. That is what Jaevery was about to face as the number two weak side linebacker and starter on some special teams. Jaevery is now traveling to away games and going to the team hotel for home games. You have to learn how to interact in these setting so that it translates to a good performance on the field. Doing things right is also important because as you grow in the program you are going to be looked upon to reciprocate what you learned to the incoming young players. These were things Jaevery and I would discuss at length. I would tell him to always watch the upper classmen that were handling themselves the right way because soon that was going to be him.

As the season got underway, Jaevery enjoyed how everything was going. The team was winning under the first year head coach. Jaevery was playing on special teams a lot, but I thought, from a father's perspective; he should have been playing in the linebacker rotation base on what I saw during fall camp. Two of Jaevery's friends were first time starters as sophomores at the outside linebacker positions. A senior was the only linebacker with any kind of experience and he was starting. The development of a player happens faster when a coach shows that he trust and believe in the player. Jaevery had just went through fall camp practicing against your number one offense, the team that was playing on Saturday, but he couldn't get quality reps against the weekly opposition. That was baffling to me. The scores use to be out of hand in favor of the university that Jaevery played for and Jaevery's two sophomore friends would finish the games. Why not give Jaevery two or three series in the last quarter to create some confidence. It's early in the season; you never know when you are going to need your second team players. These types of scenarios went on throughout the season. The opportunity to develop not only Jaevery, but Jaevery's roommate, who was also from Florida, was lost throughout the 2006 season. Jaevery and his roommate should have been used every game. The three starters played well, but Jaevery and his roommate would not have hurt the defense at all if they were inserted at any time in any game. As a coach or a defensive coordinator it's what you do. You have two true sophomores and two redshirt freshmen that are all hungry. You know they can all play; you find a way to get these players playing time and make them all happy especially when your team is winning by a large margin late in the fourth quarter. They should have been told each player in order for this team to be as good as it can be all four of you are going to have to step your games up and help this team win. This was another area where Jaevery had to deal with understanding the process. The pastor, friend, psychiatrist, educator, professor and father in me were used more than ever. I was taught that you battle not against flesh and blood, but against principalities, against powers, rulers of darkness and spiritual wickedness in high places. I stayed in prayer during this time. I knew that God had a plan for Jaevery. My main thought concerning what was happening was to keep Jaevery from becoming discouraged. When you put dis in front of the word courage the word courage loses its power. Dis in front of any word take power away from that word. The enemy (devil) knows that if he can get you discourage everything else he wants you to do, which is fail, is going to happen. Because when you are discouraged, you make bad choices and bad decisions. Another one of my quotes to Jaevery was make good choices and good decisions.

The university that Jaevery played for ended the season with a record of 11-1. They received another Capitol One bowl berth, this time against the University of Arkansas Razorbacks. Again, bowl game preparation gives the coaches time to work with the under classmen. The coaches also look at this time as a jump start to spring practice. The evaluation process allows them to see what kind of depth they are going to be working with. Talking to Jaevery during this time the conversations consisted of taking advantage of all the reps that he would get and making good choices and decisions. Bowl time is also a time when young men do a lot of things that they would later regret. You would always see on T.V. where a player would get arrested or violated some other team infraction and be suspended from the bowl game. I would remind Jaevery to be extremely careful and think good thoughts. Plus the game was in Florida two and a half hours away from our home in Orlando, Florida. Family and friends would be there.

As game day approached, I got this feeling that Jaevery was going to get some substantial and critical playing time. The last three nights before I hung up the phone, I would tell Jaevery to really focus on his alignment and assignment and that he was going to be needed in the game. The night before the game, I told Jaevery that I saw him in the game and the ball was going to come to him and he had to be ready for it. Game time came and late in the first quarter, Jaevery's team blocked a punt. Jaevery was in perfect position to scoop the ball and maybe score. Rushing, not bending down far enough, and the ball taking an awkward bounce and turn, Jaevery miss the ball. Jaevery's team did recover the fumble, but Jaevery missed an opportunity to make a play. That was what I was trying to get him to envision in our nightly conversations. As the game went on, one of the starting outside linebackers started to cramp up. Jaevery was called on to fill in. The defensive coordinator showed big time confidence in Jaevery with that move. He could have put the senior linebacker at weakside linebacker and put Jaevery's roommate in the middle. Jaevery's roommate had played more during the year and he was the senior linebacker's heir apparent the following season. You're talking about a redshirt freshman that didn't play that much during the year, Jaevery, playing against three eventual number one draft picks. Felix Jones, Darren McFadden and Tony Ugoh were on that team. Jaevery played well and finished with three tackles. He had a personal foul for hitting a receiver while he was out of bounds. Replay showed that was a good tackle and the receiver was still in bounds. The linebacker that Jaevery replaced returned to the game and Jaevery's team defeated the Razorbacks 17-14. The win was saved by an open field touchdown saving tackle on McFadden by a speedy cornerback on Jaevery's team. After the game we visited Jaevery at the team hotel. He and I talked after he was through getting hugs and kisses from his mother, aunts, uncles, friends and coaches. We talked about the missed opportunity on the blocked punt. He said he wanted to make that play so bad that he rushed himself. He then asked me overall how did I look? I told him that replay showed that was a good hit on the sideline and that he looked like he belonged out on the field. I continued to talk about the experience he gained and how it should propel him into spring ball and the 2007 season. I ended the conversation with a hug, and I'm proud of you and an I love you. Driving back to the hotel my wife and I were staying at, I couldn't help but think how much better Jaevery could have been if he would have been in the linebacker rotation throughout the season. When he was needed he was able to respond. But, how much better he could have been if he could have played in some of those blowouts win? Better reaction, recognition and pre-snap understanding.

OVERCOMING ADVERSITY

Jaevery returned home after the bowl game and stayed for the three weeks. He loved this time at home during the Florida winter compared to the chilling weather in Madison. We would work on his strength and conditioning along with doing linebacker drills. Our thoughts were, get stronger and faster and be a beast when spring practices rolled around. Jaevery's mother also loved this time. It allowed her to cook him breakfast, lunch and dinner. Not to mentions to give him a mother's hug or kiss on the cheek. Throughout this time we would always fine time to pray. Prayer keeps you ahead of all advisaries. I would talk to Jaevery about thinking God for the little things in life. I would tell him to remember when he was playing football at the recreation center and how now he is playing in front of 84,000 people. Sometimes more people depending on the team he was playing against. I would always emphasize how bless he was and for him to remember that God is the controller of all things.

Jaevery returned to the Midwest City, resumed classes and strength and conditioning. The winters were something he said he could never get used to. He always said he didn't think he ever would. The year before was a record breaking winter with lows that had not been seen in decades.

Enduring this type of weather was not an easy task. Riding a scooter in that cold Midwest winter took perseverance. When you are on your own and making your own decisions it would be easy to stay in bed and miss a class or two, which I'm sure Jaevery did, but he got up and went to enough to where his grades or his eligibility wasn't affected. On the football field is not the only place where you have to overcome adversity. Life and the things that it brings test your faith as well as your character. Who would think that the weather would and could play a part in weather a young person would stay in college or go home? This never was an issue for Jaevery, but it could be for someone who read this book. Just another area to talk about when you sign that scholarship. Obstacles come in all forms, but they are overcome the same way and that's by facing them head on with integrity and personal fortitude. Jaevery's knee started to swell up about the size of a grapefruit after he would finish with his workouts. The doctors stated that there were no structure damage and they would keep him out of some drills during his workout sessions. During this time the indoor Big Ten Track Championship was being held in the Midwest City where Jaevery played. My niece ran track for the University of Illinois, so me my wife, my niece's mother and another one of my sisters took the trip up to support my niece and see Jaevery. My wife was very happy, it gave her a reason to come and see Jaevery and she could cook for him. My main reason for going was I got the opportunity to speak with the doctors about Jaevery's knee. We enjoyed the track meet, but my niece sustained and injury and couldn't finish the meet. The time we all shared together was a good time for me. Two of my mom's offspring watching their offspring in the midst of fulfilling their dreams. We took plenty of pictures to remember those times. When I visited with the doctors, they reiterated what they said before about no structure damage. They also said that Jaevery should not think about playing beyond college. I heard what the doctors told me but, I never talked to Jaevery about what they said. The doctor can give the diagnosis, but God control the prognosis. The power of life and death is in your tongue. A father is supposed to speak blessing over his children. I know without the shadow of a doubt that the reason Jaevery was where he was had to do with me and my wife speaking blessings to Jaevery. My wife would always tell me, no matter what happen Jaevery was going to college. While she was pregnant we would talk about it. Jaevery would hear that from both of us all the time. I wasn't about to tell him what a doctor, who didn't care what the effects of his word would have had on Jaevery, said.

Throughout the rest of strength and conditioning workouts, Jaevery's workout was less pounding on his knees. The knee would still swell up and Jaevery would continue getting treatment. Spring practices 2007 came and the knee would still swell up. This was his time to shine, so he wasn't thinking about missing any practices. Just another area where he had to overcome adversity. We always talked about being tough and now was the time to display it. He didn't want to relinquish what he worked so hard to obtain. Jaevery's confidence is very high now; he had tasted a little success by playing in the game against Arkansas. Plus I was always telling him he was the best in the world. In the practices he was getting good reviews from the coaches. He would make a mistake here, make a mistake there, but overall a solid weak side or strong side linebacker. His mistakes still came with few choice curse words from the head coach or the defensive coordinator. During the spring game Jaevery played well against the number one offense. Physicality and toughness displayed. The star players only played the first half so Jaevery finished the game with a mixture of other players with the first team defense and he played very well. Not only was he making plays, but he was alignment and assignment sharp. To be a good defense and a good defensive player, you have to know where you're supposed to be. After the game, Jaevery met his mom and me in the meet and greet area. We talked with the head coach and the defensive coordinator and they were happy with Jaevery's progress and couldn't wait until fall practice started. Jaevery and I talked about how he played as we ate the wonderful food that was prepared. I told him if he was playing that way on one knee how much better would he be when he was one hundred percent. That knee was the size of a grapefruit again. Jaevery continued to get treatment on his knee until he returned home for the summer. While home, Jaevery would continue to work out then ice his knee after the workouts. We would continue to have what I was calling skull sessions. These were now man to man talks now. On Father's Day of '07, I told Jaevery that I was going to start calling him every night. The Holy Spirit showed me that that was what the devil wanted when I called myself giving Jaevery his freedom; it was just what the devil wanted us to do. Not to communicate with each other for days at a time. I told Jaevery if we just said hi and good night that would be enough. Sometimes I had to leave a message, but I called every night. It's funny how you can't talk man to man without involving women. I would always tell Jaevery that the best way I felt that he could reach his goals was to not get serious with any young lady. I would tell him about when you are sexually involved with a young lady or a woman that you are also dealing with that person's spirit. That you don't need multiple spirits depending on you to satisfy them. Concentrate on getting your goals met. I would talk to him about how relationships are time consuming and time demanding. Sometimes talking is not enough and you have to experience things for yourself. Jaevery is now twenty years old and the woman is twenty five. Jaevery tells me about how this woman really likes him and want a serious relationship with him. They were physically involve and had been seeing each other for about seven months. He wasn't interested in taking the relationship any further, but the woman didn't want to hear that. He would ask me how to end this. We talked and I told him that he should call her up and put her on speaker phone. When she asked him questions I would write down what he should say. Their conversation went on for about fifteen minutes, her talking, me writing and Jaevery telling her what I wrote. The woman then said," Jaevery this don't sound like you, who have you been talking to"? Jaevery kept his composure and said this is how I feel. My words pertaining to her were basically you have reached your goal; you are a professional woman with a career. If you care for me like you say you do allow me to reach my goals without the extra pressure of a committed relationship. The woman didn't go quietly, but they eventually parted ways. This was another area where adversity had to be overcome, even though it was personally induced. The overall maturation process concerning academics, athletics and his personal life wasn't going that bad. You would want everything to be trouble free, but life is just not that way. I saw a lot of resolve and personal fortitude in Jaevery the summer of 2007. He was becoming that young man that I envisioned. He still had some rough edges that he had to smooth out, but I could see him maturing. One morning, Jaevery came out of his room and I stopped him and told him that I wanted to pray for him. When we held hands the Holy Spirit was on me so strong that all I could do was cry. I must have cried for about five minutes. I couldn't get a word out of my mouth. Jaevery was holding me saying" its okay daddy, it's okay"," it's going to be alright". Finally, being able to talk, I talk to Jaevery about not allowing bad choices and bad decision to ruin what he had going for him. Not to allow what God had blessed him with to be looked upon as something you could just squander. I told him young black men don't always get second chances when they make a mistake. I poured my heart out to him about how much I loved him and how much God love him to allow this to be happing to him, and then I prayed. When we talked later that morning, Jaevery stated he didn't know what was wrong with me when I was crying, but he felt good the whole time.

Jaevery left for summer classes and strength and conditioning. The conversations now deal with being focus, not letting a day go by that you don't work hard, things like that. I would text him things like how is the best linebacker in the country doing. He would say,"O.K. Thanks daddy". This would go on all summer. I had to come up with ways to keep him motivated and hungry even though fall camp was a couple months away. The knee would still swell up after every workout and Jaevery continued getting treatment on it. Classes were going fine and there was some female drama, but nothing outlandish. Fall camp 2007 started with Jaevery second on the depth chart behind the starter the previous year. The knee was still and issue, but Jaevery wouldn't allow that to keep him out of practice. When I would talk to him he would tell me he doesn't even think about his knee. He would say I'm going to practice hard then get treatment. After several practices, the starting strong side linebacker suffered a hamstring injury. Jaevery was move to strong side linebacker with the first team defense. There was approximately two and a half to three weeks of practices left before the season opening game. On the days leading to my arrival in that Midwest City, the websites and coaches were talking about how Jaevery was looking good and how he was really taking advantage of that opportunity to be with the first team defense. When I would talk to him at night he would tell me that he is feeling more comfortable every practice. He would talk about how he was making tackles in the backfield, making interception, getting his hands on balls and how well he was covering the tight ends. During fall camp the team has a Family Day. This is an event where families bring their kids to the stadium and they can participate in multiple activities and get autographs from coaches and players. The weather was unusually hot that day and when Jaevery showed up, he had a t-shirt wrapped around his head and it looked like a doorag. This rubbed the head coach the wrong way and Jaevery was given some choice words that were related to Jaevery coming into this event looking like a gang member. There was also an article where I felt the head coach put his own spin on the content of the article. During these practices the defense had been really given it to the offense and when they scored they would taunt or do a dance. The head coach wanted this to stop. Before the head coach put a halt to all celebrations, Jaevery intercepted a pass, scored the touchdown and threw the ball in the stands. A couple practices (days) later Jaevery intercepted another pass and scored. This time he did a break dance in the end zone with a funky spin. The head coach told the reporter that Jaevery was immature and he had a lot of growing up to do. His immaturity had something to do with why he wasn't playing a lot. My wife and I read this and we both were very upset. I was leaving to come to that Midwest City the morning that I read that article. My wife said I'm going to e-mail the head coach and tell him how I feel. First I told her no don't do that. I was thinking Jaevery is already not playing that much and we don't need to do anything to put him further behind. Then I thought about it a little more. I read the article again and again. I saw that the head coach put his spin on the article. The reporter didn't ask how mature was Jaevery McFadden? The reporter ask," was it a good thing that Jaevery McFadden was taking advantage of the starting strong side linebacker being out"? The head coach chose to talk about Jaevery walking in an event looking like a gang member, break dancing in the end zone and being immature. I gave my wife the okay to send the e-mail. The head coach was in his second year and he was new to his overall craft. I felt this would be a good opportunity for him to check himself. Even if it only made him think a little bit, at least it made him think. Speak on the questions ask, don't always coach's speak when the questions are obvious. Coaches speak gives coaches reasons to not play a player that they don't want to play. I arrived in the Midwest City to watch the last two weeks of practices and the opening game. I usually talk to the head coach before or after practice while on the field during the first practice I attend. The defensive coordinator approached me at the beginning of practice and asked me how I was doing and how was the family. When I'm asked how the family is it's about how is the wife. Jaevery is an only child. The defensive coordinator is not worrying about how my mother, brothers or sisters are doing he didn't even know them. I could tell the defensive coordinator was trying to feel me out and that he was aware of the e-mail my wife sent the head coach. He wanted to see if I was angry or had ill feelings toward the head coach. The fact that I was in town right after my wife e-mailed the head coach, means I'm here to get some straightening on why Jaevery was labeled that way in the newspaper. I told him I was okay and the wife was doing well. We small talked about how well Jaevery was playing and he went on the field to get ready for practice. The head coach came on the field and got involved with practice as I sat in the bleachers and watched. I saw him and the defensive coordinator talking to each other, but I didn't make much of it. Jaevery had another good practice with the number one defense at strong side linebacker. He was still feeling in for the starting strong side linebacker who was rehabbing his hamstring injury. This was my third fall camp and I had been to two spring practice sessions and games. The players were becoming more familiarized with me every time I came in town. After every practice I would get a pound (handshake) from all the linebackers, defensive backs, linemen, coaches you name it. Mostly all the players and coaches were receptive to me. Steve, head of security, and I became good friends. Coach M would ask me if I had a home in that Midwest City because for someone who stayed in Florida I was up there a lot. I remember all the linebackers approaching me and the weak side linebacker saying, "Your boy is doing his thing", talking about Jaevery. Jaevery's roommate yelled out "he should be starting". The starting strong side linebacker was standing there and heard every word. I pounded and hugged them and told them all that I would talk to them later. Jaevery had gained the respect of his teammates. It had become obvious to them that Jaevery was one of the best linebackers on the defense. You know that you have arrived when your teammates know that you are good. It should have been a wrap for the coaches to see it. The head coach did welcome me in town and he told me that he got an e-mail from my wife. He talked about how the culture is in the Midwest and the perception the program would get if he allowed doorags to be worn. A couple days later in the sports section of the newspaper the superstar starting cornerback was there with a red doorag on. Go figure! He made his case for everything that he said in the newspaper. I just listened to him as though I didn't know anything. I left him thinking that my wife wrote that e-mail without my knowledge. The reason that I did that was because from my perspective, the head coach was the type of person that would hold a grudge. It was 2007 and I knew that around draft time 2010 that would come back to hunt Jaevery.

I based that on my ability to discern people and I do that very well.

As the season opening game drew near, Jaevery continued to be effective in every practice. The strong side linebacker has to be a good run stopper at the point of attack and has to be able to cover the tight end. What I was witnessing was a player who was ready to explode on the scene. What we talked about all spring and summer concerning taking his game to another level was about to happen. Jaevery's mentality was that I'm a starter and I'm going to make it hard for the coaches not to start me. After one of the practices, I drove Jaevery to his apartment. I had witnessed about a week of practices and what I was seeing Jaevery do didn't surprise me. I was just happy he was getting the chance to prove it to himself that he could do it. While in the elevator I told him that I was watching a first round draft pick. I know I'm speaking from a father's perspective, but if it was anybody else playing that way, I would have made the same assessment. Jaevery was playing that well. The Wednesday before the season opening game, one of the team doctors saw me standing on the sideline after practice. He told me to tell Jaevery to be ready to start because the injured strong side linebacker was about a week or two away from being ready to play. When I saw the injured strong side linebacker working out with the trainers that assessment looked right. He was still noticeably dragging his leg. I talked to Jaevery about what the doctor said and he said the coaches were telling him the same thing.

Game time came and the injured strong side linebacker was in the starting lineup. It was so obvious that he was still hurting by the way he played, moved and ran. I watched the injured strong side linebacker on every play and I thought if they can't trust Jaevery now than when will they. With all due respect to the injured strong side linebacker, he looked terrible out there. Jaevery only played on special teams during the game. Jaevery was devastated when we talked after the game. He stated to me "daddy what else can I do"? He went on to say "if they think the injured strong side linebacker is better than me on one leg then what's left for me to do." Jaevery thought his play in fall camp should have at least given the coaches enough confidences in him to where they could have allowed the injured strong side linebacke to get one hundred percent ready. How much worse Jaevery could have played if he had been given the opportunity? He had displayed that he could handle the position by the way he played against the number one and number two offenses on his team. At a time when the coaches could have created depth at the outside linebacker positions they gave in to star treatment and allowed a player to play that never should have been nowhere near the field. Not only what was done was wrong, but the coaches didn't leave Jaevery in a good football state of mind. As a coach you have to be able to make those kinds of moves without losing a player. I had to really comfort Jaevery during this time. I talked to him about recapturing his focus and drive. His focus on playing special team had wavered. I told him that special teams were all he had right now. We talked about this was another chance to make lemonade out of the lemon that he was given. It was also another time in Jaevery's life where he had to overcome adversity. As a father, I was hurting inside. When your son hurt and you had no way of making it right, prayer was again my defense mechanism. This was another opportunity to use my pastor, psychiatrist, psychologist, professor, educator, and friend skills that I had learned over the years. Although I was hurting I still knew who my source was. Getting Jaevery to realize that this too shall pass was my main concern. He did talk about transferring, but that was nipped in the bud very quickly. I told him what he could do somewhere else he could accomplish the same thing here. I reminded him about the time he played little league baseball. After two games he wanted to quit. I told him he didn't have to play baseball anymore after that season was over, but he had to finish that season. I went on to talk about how he stuck it out and if I would had allowed him to quit then he would be looking for me to make it easy for him now. By midseason, Jaevery had his focus back and begin to make plays. I can recall a play he made in Happy Valley against Penn State where he caused a fumble on a punt return. He had also started coming in on third down at the middle linebacker position in the 3-3-5 defensive package. Jaevery had his swag back and it showed. He help the defense get off the field a lot by making plays on third down. I'm thinking if you can play on third down, you can definitely play on first and second. The team that Jaevery played for had a game against the Illini in Champagne. Jaevery's roommate, who was the starting linebacker, was involved in an incident where a motor scooter was stolen. Jaevery's roommate would travel to the game but, he didn't play. This was a chance to get your three best linebackers on the field and the coaches went with another young linebacker and not start Jaevery. Nothing against the other young linebacker, but Jaevery had displayed that he was ready to start at any of the linebacker positions. The way he played in the Arkansas game, how well he played in fall camp and he was playing middle linebacker in the third down package should have made starting him a no brainer. The young linebacker that started hadn't had that many snaps up to that point. The physicality that was needed in that game was standing on the sideline wearing number 47 and his name is Jaevery McFadden. Mendenhall dominated that game running up the middle and with screen plays. I don't know how much better Jaevery would have played, but I wish I would have gotten the chance to see. The coaches could have at least rotated them. Jaevery's team would go on to lose that game. Jaevery had begun to take advantage of all the playing time he was getting whether it was special teams or the third down package.

The game against Northern Illinois was the game that would change Jaevery's season. On the Monday and Tuesday before that game I found myself pondering whether or not I would go to that game. I needed to make a decision quick because my wife needed time to get a good rate on a ticket. On Thursday in my spirit the Holy Spirit told me to go "Jaevery need to see you". I arrived in that Midwest City on Friday morning. When I got to the field Steve was there and was glad to see me as usual. The defensive coordinator came on the field and he told me how excited he was to see Jaevery play this week and he thought he would play well. The practices on Fridays aren't that long. After practice Jaevery came over to me with a look in his eye that I remembered seeing when he was ten years old. That look said, that's my dad! The look reminded me of when he was younger. Jaevery always showed me and told me he was glad that I was his father. That look said it all. We gave each other a pound and a hug before I was swarmed by the other players. The head coach came and said hi as Jaevery and I walked to the locker room. Jaevery told me he was glad to see me and that he needed that visit. I told him that the Holy Spirit prompted me to come and the look in his eyes when he saw me told it all. I talked to him about what the defensive coordinator told me and he said he was happy with the packages he was in. He couldn't wait for the game.

During the first quarter of the game, Jaevery was playing well in the 3-3-5 scheme. He was helping the defense get off the field on third down and really looking good out there. I remember a nice play he made on a screen play where he had a six yard tackle for loss. As the half was ending T.D. threw an interception. The defense had to come on the field again. Northern Illinois ran a pass play and Jaevery was blitzing the quarterback.

Jaevery had a straight beeline toward the quarterback, but the right tackle lunged and cut Jaevery's legs from under him. Trying to break his fall, Jaevery fell in a way that the pressure was too much and it dislocated his right elbow. I saw the whole play and knew it was serious if Jaevery was coming off the field. He was too tough not to stay on the field if the injury was minor. While Jaevery was walking off the field I ask the angels and the Holy Spirit to move on Jaevery's behalf concerning the injury. The team went in for halftime and I waited to see if Jaevery would come out in a brace, a sling or whatever. When the team returned for the second half Jaevery had his arm in a sling. Jaevery's team would go on to win the game. After the game I was with Jaevery when he was talking to the doctors. The first diagnosis was the bursa sac in his right elbow had burst. That type of injury would've allowed him to come back and play the following week. After getting an MRI, ligament damage was found. It was stated by the doctors and the head coach that Jaevery's elbow came out of the socket, but he somehow put it back in place. I believe that the angels and the Holy Spirit responded to my prayer and that that was another reason I had to be at that game. Northern Illinois was a game that I would not have gone to in a million years, but the Holy Spirit knows best. Jaevery missed the next three games against Indiana, Ohio State and Michigan. During the rehab, I talked to him about using that time to reflect on his journey and recharge his battery. Lemonade out of a lemon again. Another chance to overcome adversity. We talked about how if you don't go through anything you will never find out who you are. I would also reiterate my experiences to him. I told him that the reason that I had answers to all his questions and situations was because I had been through those types of situations and more. Jaevery was never the type of kid that was hard to convince something was right. He was where he was because he believed it would happen. Anything that I told Jaevery he believed it and I liked that. He really trusted in what I said. I think that is a good trait for a young man to have concerning the wisdom of his father. He believed in Santa Claus until he was eleven years old. I have him on VCR talking about how Santa Claus ate and drank the cookies and milk he left out.

Jaevery returned to the Minnesota game and helped his team secure the Paul Bunyan Ax for the fourth consecutive year. He played with a big brace on his elbow. He made some plays, but he was just happy to be back on the field with his teammates. That was the last game of the season and it gave Jaevery time to try and recapture his rhythm while practicing for the Outback bowl against the University of Tennessee. Bowl game practices are times when you can refresh yourself and refocus, especially if you are coming off an injury. This game was being play in Tampa, Florida. The drive is about three and a half hours from Riviera Beach. Family and friends will be at the game again. That would be the third year in a row that Jaevery's team had come to Florida. Our conversations during that time consisted of watching what you do; focusing on his assignments and getting proper rest. I reminded him of how he missed an opportunity to score off the blocked punt in last year Capital One bowl game. I told him somewhere during the game he would have a chance to make a big play and he had to be ready for it.

Game day arrived with family and friends in the stadium. Jaevery's team held the Volunteers on their first drive. On third down, Jaevery had a chance to make a big play. The quarterback threw the ball right to Jaevery, but he dropped the ball. He was getting his depth in his drop zone and when he turned around the ball was on him. No excuses, he should have caught that ball. It's the kind of plays that we always talked about. He could have scored if he had caught the ball. The rest of the game Jaevery played okay, nothing sparkling or jaw dropping, just consistent. The Volunteers would go on to win the game. The head coach went for a fourth and short, but Jaevery's team came up short. Jaevery's team had an opportunity to win the game if they would have kicked a field goal. A win going into the spring and the ability to build off a bowl win during the summer and fall camp was lost. That was the start of a 2008 season with much turbulence.

DON'T BELIEVE THE HYPE

After the bowl game Jaevery returned home with me and his mother. We talked about his possibilities for the 2008 season. Jaevery talked to me about the snaps he got during bowl week at the middle linebacker position. He told me that the coaches were going to give him a chance to win the position. While at home Jaevery worked hard to stay in shape. He ran up and down the beach, did his position drill work and lifted weights. He was preparing himself to have a great winter conditioning session to elevate him in the spring. We had been down that road before where you prepare yourself mentally and physically, but you don't get what you prepared for. But, this time the coaches were dealing with Jaevery as though he was needed. I can remember him saying to me," it sure is nice to feel like you are needed". Jaevery's mindset was different. He now felt like he belonged. Our conversations were where I thought they should have been during the 2006 season. You have to remember, I thought like a champion all the time. So I knew how to motivate him. Just because I never got a chance to play on the big stage didn't mean I was clueless to getting the best out of talent, especially my own son. Like I said earlier assessing talent is what I do best. Jaevery had to wait until his fouth season to see legitimate playing time and that was a shame. This is a kid that was a first team All-State utility player from Florida that was counted on to win games playing defense and offense while in high school. He knew how to play if given the opportunity. Now he was being given an honest opportunity to compete against the same players that he came in with. Coming from a father's perspective, this was two years too late. The whole 2006 season I thought every linebacker on that roster should have been rotating, Jaevery included. They were all about the same talent wise. Now all of a sudden, well I guest not all of a sudden, Jaevery can compete. These are the same players except the senior linebacker in 2006. Jaevery's work with the number one defense at both outside linebacker position from 2006 until now showed he could play those positions. His third down package play and his work during the bowl practices finally convinced the coaches that Jaevery just might be one of the three best linebackers on the team.

Until Jaevery left for winter conditioning we would have skull sessions about how he was going to attack winter conditioning and spring practices. Jaevery's mentality was, it's time to take something. He felt all along that he was just as good as any linebacker on the team. Some of his teammates thought so too. His roommate said it in front of the starting linebackers during fall camp of 2007. I continued to add fuel to his confidence by telling him it was going to be his time. That this was what he had been waiting on. My job was not only to make him feel good, but to keep it in his head that he was that good. It wasn't hard to do because Jaevery believed whatever came out of my mouth. He always knew I had his best interest at heart.

Jaevery returned for classes and winter conditioning. He was still experiencing swelling in his knee, but he didn't let it affect him. Some of his workout sessions were tapered down and he did work in the pool. I would remind him about the type of focus that was necessary to be great. We were still talking every night so I always took that opportunity to impart wisdom to him. I would talk about how God was answering our prayers. I say our prayers because I wanted to see my son's dream come true. I would tell him to look back to when the coaches changed his position to where he was now. We talked about when he cried and thought his world was ending to now feeling like he was on top of the world. I never let him feel like success would not happen. God has a way of working things out. I always told Jaevery that the head coach and the defensive coordinator did not control his destiny and that God did. With all due respect to the head coach and the defensive coordinator, they're word weren't final concerning Jaevery. I know that prayer was the reason that Jaevery was being given a chance to play. I'm not saying that I wasn't praying in 2006, because I was, but God's timing is the best timing. I thought about my visit with the head coach during the time that Jaevery's position was changed from tight end to linebacker. How I only went to his office to say hello and he told me that Jaevery was about a year or two from helping the team. That was the spring of 2006. I could have argued, disgust it or agreed to disagree with him, but I chose to listen and not say anything. I knew prayer was what I had to do to change the situation. Reflecting on the ups and downs, the adverse times and Jaevery's overall journey, gave me the chance to share with him on how God gave him the strength to persevere through each trying situation. The Bible says that no weapon that is form against you shall be able to prosper. It didn't say that the weapons would not be formed. The weapons can form all they want, but they won't prosper. I continued to encourage Jaevery all winter. Our conversations always had something to do with focus, success and being great. It made my day and night when I talked to him. It was usually between 10:15p.m. - 10:30p.m. Central time and 11:15-11:30 Eastern time when I called. I slept well after our conversations.

Spring practices 2008 were now starting and there was a shift in the plans concerning where Jaevery was going to play. The weak side linebacker sustained an injury to his hamstring during winter conditioning and he couldn't practice. Jaevery was at the weak side linebacker position with the number one defense, which scratched the competition at the middle linebacker position. We were aware that this was going to happen and we talked about making lemonade out of a lemon again. Practices went well day in and day out. On the websites the coaches were given Jaevery rave reviews. About eight days before the spring game, I arrived in that Midwest City. Again, I only come to spring practices and fall camp to assess Jaeverys progress. Now, it was a matter of feeding his confidence. Ray Charles and Stevie Wonder could see that Jaevery was one of the three best linebackers on the team now. While I was watching practice, I would envision Jaevery making the same type of big plays that he was making in practice in the games on Saturdays. Jaevery played well in all phases of practice. During the goal line drill he was tough and physical.

During seven on seven, he got his hands on balls and made interceptions. During team drills (offense against defense) he put it all together and flat out played well. The team had a lot of injuries that year. The starting tight end, running back, linemen on offense and defense each missed all or a significant amount of time during spring practice. Several players in the secondary were also out. The injured players would do drills on the sidelines with the trainers. I thought some of the players were big timing the situation. Jaevery's knee was swelling up like a grapefruit every day, but he still practiced. The mindset that was going to be needed to win games in the fall was not being cultivated during this spring session from a father's perspective. Players that were hurt on the sidelines were acting like they were better than they were. Swagger is not necessary on the sidelines. With all the players being out, the level of competition wasn't the same. Jaevery's activeness and his physicality were very apparent. After practices I would use the five to ten minutes, if that, to tell Jaevery that he was looking good on the field and for him to build off of each practice. The starting weak side linebacker would miss all the spring and Jaevery took all the reps with the first team defense. His confidence was through the roof and I loved feeding it with statements like, good better best, never settle for less, until your good is better and your better is your best. I also reminded him to keep visiting Bible verse Psalsm 119:97-100.

The spring game had some hype, but the quote unquote stars were out with injuries. The quarterback position was up for grabs again just like the previous year when T. D. beat out D. S. A. E. and D. S. were the leading candidates to win the starting job. The spring game is a game where the coaches want the players who suppose too play well, to play well. They also would love to find a couple of surprises and create some depth. The most important thing is for no one to get injured during the game. Jaevery played well in the game. His play was consistent. He made the same type of plays he had been making all spring. The coaches let him know that he had a good spring and they also told me during the meet and greet. The head coach and the defensive coordiator both expressed to me how pleased they were with the way Jaevery played. They also knew Jaevery shouldn't have been playing with the way his knee would swell up. Jaevery was tough though and I knew that. I also knew what his dream was. If he would have said daddy my knee hurt too bad and I can't go, the coaches would have been notified by me that he couldn't go and we would have moved on from there. Jaevery was mentally tough. I saw his knee after treatment. I would bring ice to his apartment for him to continue icing his knee down so that he could practice the next day. Sometimes I didn't know how he did it. But, then again I knew. God is good. When I say Jaevery shouldn't have been playing, I mean there were times that I felt the head coach thought I was going to tell him Jaevery's not playing anymore. When he talked to me at the meet and greet, he made the statement"Jaevery has to keep getting treatment on that knee". I could tell he was just looking for my reaction. He wanted me to say something, but I never did. It was obvious to me that the head coach knew that Jaevery was sacrificing himself for the team.

The summer of Jaevery's fourth year junior season was here. While home, Jaevery worked out harder than he did in previous summers when he was home. I purchased him a membership at the local L.A. Fitness. He would lift weights and swim in the pool in the morning and do his linebacker drills in the afternoon. Our conversations would be about taking his game to another level. I would tell him that what he wanted was right there before him. We talked about being prepared, attention to detail and just plain old getting after somebody. That was a good time for Jaevery. He knew that he was going to be on the field somewhere that upcoming season. The competition at middle linebacker was his main priority. He would say things like, I can't wait to get started, and it's going to be hard for the coaches not to play me this year. I was still taking every chance I got to let Jaevery know that he was great. When I spoke to him first thing in the morning, I would say, how is the best linebacker in the world doing. He would say," I'm good daddy". Jaevery ate confidence for breakfast, lunch and dinner. It was all I knew to do. After watching three seasons go by and not being a big contributing factor, Jaevery was prime and ready to compete.

Jaevery left for the 2008 summer classes and conditioning. We continued our nightly talks. I would tell him things like, I say this to you and I say it without hesitation, you don't win in the game, you win in the preparation. I would also say, your will to prepare to win has to be better than your will to win. Those little sayings and more was what I used to make sure Jaevery stayed focus. School was going okay, the female problems had subsided, and football was his main focus. From the first week of June until the first week of August the players are taking summer classes and they are working out. Camaraderie, captains, chemistry, and continuity are being developed. A lot of seven on seven is being played where the skill positions players go against the linebackers and defensive backs. Jaevery would tell me, I got a pick today or broke up three pass today. He was exuding a lot of confidence. This went on until fall camp 2008 started.

Fall camp started as well as the competition for the middle linebacker position. Jaevery and his roommate were the leading candidates, but the other young linebacker was placed in the mix. These young men were all good friends. Jaevery and his roommate were roommates for the first two years and they call themselves brothers to this day. Jaevery's roommate also still calls me pop. Our relationship grew from the time Jaevery's roommate came to our home from Ft. Lauderdale, Florida to visit Jaevery before they went off to college. I can remember Jaevery's roommate and Jaevery in Jaevery's room watching Jaevery's high lite tape of his junior and senior year in high school. When they finished watching the tape Jaevery's roommate said, "They should have recruited you to play defense, you're good". Jaevery's roommate always knew that Jaevery could play. He was the one that said Jaevery should be starting when Jaevery was filling in for the injured strong side linebacker during the 2006 fall camp.

During the first couple of practices Jaevery had to get use to the terminology, making sure others were where they were suppose too be and his own alignment and assignment. For about a week and a half Jaevery and the young linebacker went back and forth working with the first team defense. Jaevery's roommate had dropped to the third team behind another young linebacker. I think there was an off the field incidents that put Jaevery's roommate behind the other players. The coaches were worried about if they could trust him or not. There were days that Jaevery played lights out and there were days when he wasn't as sharp. The websites were reporting quotes from the coaches stating Jaevery was taking advantage of the opportunity he was being given. They talked about how he was making tackles all over the field. Another website would talk about how Jaevery needed to make sure he understood the schemes. That being fast and not knowing where you supposed to be wasn't good. With about two weeks left in camp, Jaevery and the young linebacker were still alternating with the number one defense. It was time that someone solidified themselves and made the position theirs. I arrived in that Midwest City on a Thursday morning. I would watch the remaining practices and the first two games at the stadium. The Wednesday before I arrived, Jaevery was on top of his game. He was making the right calls, making tackles all over the field and very effective in the passing game. The website said he had two interceptions that day and broke up several passes. The defensive coordinator made the statement that whoever plays the best at Thursday's practice would be declared the starter. I got to practice about thirty minutes before the players came out. Steve greeted me and we chatted it up a little. The players started coming on the field and I would get the usual handshake, hug and how have you been doing. When Jaevery came through and we saw each other, I saw that gleam in his eyes. It made me think of when he was younger again. He had that "that's my daddy" look on his face. We hugged quickly and I told him to impress me as he walked over to get stretched out. Saying impress me to Jaevery goes back to Jaevery's high school days. Those were the last two words he heard from me before he went on the field to play. I would tell him that because if he could impress me that meant he played big time. He needed another big time performance that day so I thought I would stir up the juices. He was playing well, but now it was time to leave no doubt in the coaches mind that he and he alone was the player that should be the starting middle linebacker for his 2008 team. That practice Jaevery's game went to the level that I had envisioned. He did the things that I always thought he could do. He had three interceptions throughout the practice. Two of them he dove and caught. He made tackles in the holes and behind the line of scrimmage. He couldn't be blocked. I mean he was sideline to sideline making tackles. I sat there in the stadium as proud as I could be. Jaevery was out there earning the respect of his teammates and his coaches. After that practice, I can remember defensive back coach K. C. and defensive line coach R. Mc. telling me how well Jaevery had been playing all camp. They were very impressed. Yes, he impressed me too.

 I talked to the head coach and the defensive coordinator after that practice and they each praised Jaevery to me about his play during that camp and that particular practice. They were mostly concerned with him making the right calls. The middle linebacker has to know what to do when the formation change from the pre-set read. He has to translate that to his linemen and other linebackers. The safeties make the calls for the secondary. Everybody has to be on the same page. With Jaevery's athleticism he was able to make up for his mistakes when he didn't line up in the right position. Lining up and being where you supposed to be was what the coaches needed Jaevery to be consistent at, they knew he could make plays. He put it all together that practice and made the decision easy for the coaches.

Jaevery was named the starting middle linebacker after that practice. That team had major hype all spring, summer and all fall camp long. They were ranked number five in the country with several first team All-Big Ten players on that team. The offense was led by A. E. at quarterback, P. J. H. at running back and T.B. at tight end. The defense was led by a defensive line that returned four starters in M. S., M. N., J. C. and a defensive end pass rush extraordinaire. The starting weak side and strong side linebackers also returned along with starters in the secondary. Jaevery's roommate returned, but was in the coach's dog house. But you could see why that team was ranked in the top ten in the country. Depth was everywhere, but at the defensive line position and that position was about to take a hit that the team would never recover from. The next practice, which was the Friday that ended camp, the team would lose its pass rush extraordinaire defensive end who could line up on both defensive end position and rush the quarterback. Practice had ended and the team had circled up or huddled up to listen to the head coach speak. I didn't hear the beginning of the head coach speech to the team because I was a nice distance away on the sidelines. But, all of a sudden the players started to scatter around trying to keep the pass rushing extraordinaire away from the head coach. The head coach was walking toward the tunnel where the players come on the field to practice, but he was still on the field. The pass rushing extraordinaire was yelling some very explicit word to the head coach. It should be noted that the head coach is Caucasian and the pass rush extraordinaire is an African- American. The pass rush extraordinaire was telling the head coach "you can't coach anyway!" I heard the head coach say "but this is my team and I'm not going to let you ruin it". The head coach also yelled some explicit words before yelling "I tried to help you 'young man," I'm not going to let you mess this team up." The players were doing their best trying to keep the pass rushing extraordinaire away from the head coach and at the same time trying to direct him toward the locker room. The pass rushing extraordinaire continued with his verbal barrage. He stated to coach Mc. as he was walking through the tunnel, "y'all know that he can't coach," y'all just scared of his ass". He then said the same thing to the defensive coordinator as he was walking through the tunnel. The players were even trying to put their hands over the pass rushing extraordinaire's mouth. While the pass rushing extraordinaire was saying those words, I was standing about fifteen yards away from the head coach and he wasn't saying anything. The players were able to escort the pass rushing extraordinaire to the locker room. I walked with Jaevery to the locker room and I asked him," where did all that come from"? Jaevery told me that the head coach thought the pass rushing extraordinaire was talking while he was talking and asked the pass rushing extraordinaire did he have anything to say. The pass rushing extraordinaire said he didn't and the incident escalated from there. During this whole argument you could tell that the pass rushing extraordinaire was intoxicated. Why did it happen? I don't know. Should it have happened, from a father's perspective, I have to say no. What I witnessed was a coach who hadn't been challenged in that manner before or if he had been he didn't learn anything from it. Almost the whole program was there on the field that day. Equipment managers, trainers, security, players and coaches were all on the field. Everybody was there except the athletic director and his brass. When you are in a position where you are the leader of young men, you don't conduct yourself in that manner. The pass rushing extraordinaire was given ammunition to use by the head coach trying to demean him in front of the team. Some players a coach can get away with that with and there are players like the pass rushing extraordinaire that you can't do that with. Although the pass rushing extraordinaire was wrong with what he said and by being intoxicated at practice, the coaches could have kept that incident in house. The coaches can keep what they want out of the media. Jaevery's roommate was home in Ft. Lauderdale the summer of his redshirt freshman year. He was supposed to be back in that Midwest City on a Sunday before classes and conditioning started. He went to South Beach (Miami) on Friday and was caught with marijuana. The first person he called was me. He was crying and afraid that the head coach was going to kick him off the team or suspend him for a period of time. I told him he had to tell the coaches and let the chips fall where they may. When the coaches got this news it never made it to the media. Jaevery's roommate was at that time one of the programs prize recruits. The athletic director was also aware of that incident. That incident never made it to the media.

The coaches and the athletic director made a decision to keep the incident from the media because, again from a father's perspective, Jaevery's roommate at that time was a recruit that the coaches was high on and if the media got a hold of that information the coaches would have had to make a decision that would have affected Jaevery's roommate's eligibility. From a father's perspective, the way the head coach should have handled that incident was he should have asked the pass rushing extraordinaire, no, he should have told the pass rushing extraordinaire to get with his position coach and the defensive coordinator and meet him in his office right then. There they could have cussed, fussed and argued all night, but when the meeting was over, the pass rushing extraordinaire would have still been on the team. This was and in house incident. That practice was closed to the media. I was the only spectator in the stadium. I think the head coach made a prideful and hasty decision. You have to let your emotion subside before you decide to do things that are going to affect you and other people. The coaches had the players vote to see if the pass rushing extraordinaire would be kept on the team. I don't know how close the voting was and neither did Jaevery, but the pass rushing extraordinaire was kicked off the team. Some players that weren't going to play a down all year voted to keep your number one pass rusher off the team. I guarantee you if you would have let the three deep vote they would have kept him on the team. The pass rushing extraordinaire would've made both defensive tackles and the other defensive end job that much easier. Not to mention a new middle linebacker (Jaevery) and already being short on the defensive line. The non-productive secondary's play that year was because there was no pass rush. That pass rushing extraordinaire was a fifth year senior that knew the defense very well and was also good as a run stopper. He also was tough and would have put a foot in the pre-Madonna tight end and running back and anybody else's but that was slacking. The pass rushing extraordinaire didn't tear his ACL and missed his senior season; he had a run in with the head coach. The head coach was to prideful. You just don't lose a player that talented that way. No way is he kicked off of my team. He would have run the stadium stairs at five in the morning or some other type of early morning discipline until I was satisfied, but he would have played for me. He owed me, the coaches and his teammates that. I was being told that the pass rushing extraordinaire did what many other players wanted to do, but not with that type of racism. But there were some players during that time that thought the head coach didn't handle them the right way either.

Not having the pass rushing extraordinaire was the beginning of a season that didn't live up to the hype it received. The first two games of the season Jaevery was leading the team in tackles with twenty tackles. He had twelve against Akron and eight against Marshall. During the next game against Fresno State, right before half time Jaevery made a tackle and he broke a bone in his right hand. Jaevery returned after the half with a club on his hand and finished the game. He would have surgery that following Tuesday, 9-16-08, going into the bye week. The reason that I remember the date so well is because my wife's car over heated in our garage. It was about five in the evening. My wife had returned from work at about four thirty with my nephew, who she tutored. They were in the back room on the computer. I was laying down taking a nap. My wife would tell me later that something told her to go check the garage. The Holy Spirit is good! When she got there she could smell smoke. I heard her scream my name, "John there is smoke in the garage"! I jumped up thinking this was something I could just spit on and put out. When I opened the garage door, the smoke rushed in through the den area of the house letting me know it was time to get her and my nephew out of the house. Fire was coming from the engine area of my wife's car. This was nothing I could spit on and put out, 911 were called and they dispatched a fire truck. We all got out safe and watched as the firemen hosed down every inch of the house. Smoke filled every room before the firemen could arrive. My wife's car was destroyed and my sports utility vehicle was destroyed. Pictures of Jaevery when he was small, trophies and clothing all destroyed. When Jaevery got out of surgery he would have to here that type of news. I remember telling him and he asked me do I need him to come home. I quickly told him to take care of things where he is and I'll take care of things here at home. Jaevery and adversity again, he could handle it. Club on my hand and now everything in my parent's home is destroyed. God is still good though. That's what I would tell Jaevery. Don't worry about anything at home; God is still in control of this family. Jaevery played seven straight games with that club on his hand and the remaining games he wore a protective brace. He did not miss a game. The starting middle linebacker playing with a club on his hand was an honorable thing. But, Jaevery would tell me after every game that he left at least five to six plays on the field that he should have made. I could tell teams would game plan to run at him and to block him on his left side leaving the hand with the club free. That made it hard for Jaevery to tackle. Toughness was displayed by Jaevery every week. He would tell me that every time that hand hit anything the pain was excruciating. He said it hurt even worst when they lost. Michigan beat them in a tale of two halves game. The pre-Madonna tight end should have played that whole game instead of waiting till late in the fourth quarter trying to be a hero in the last part of the game. When he was out there he looked pretty healthy to me. He was out of the game up to that time due to a hamstring pull quote un quote. The lost to Ohio State was also a bad lost. Players running around like chickens with their heads cut off on defense during that last drive. The coaches didn't perform well on that last play. They took too long getting the defensive call to Jaevery and the rest of the defense. Terrell Pryor scored around the left end untouched. Jaevery's team would also go on to lose to Penn State, Iowa and Michigan State. The hype was fleeting, now the word was overrated. Players played not to get hurt and some were too worried about their draft status in the NFL. A team that should have easily been no worse than 10-2 ended up playing for their bowl bid lives against a division II school in Cal Poly. That game went into overtime and Jaevery's team was able to win when Cal Poly's kicker missed an extra point. That kicker missed three extra points that game. That game the defensive coordinator started the other young linebacker at middle linebacker instead of Jaevery. The reason he gave was because the other young linebacker played against a team that ran the veer offense in high school. The veer was the same offense that Cal Poly ran with several different variations. They also had a big time receiver that gave Jaevery's team best cornerback and the rest of the secondary a fit that day. Jaevery played against teams that ran the option in high school too. From a father's perspective, I was livid. The last game of the season and you don't start a kid that had given you everything he had. He played all year with one hand for you and that was how you rewarded him by telling him the other young linebacker played against an offense like this in high school so he's starting this week, unbelievable. Not to mention still getting treatment on his knee after every practice and game. Jaevery made a lot of key stops in that game that was instrumental in the win. If he would have started, he probably would have had a monster game.

Jaevery's team finished the season 7-5 and receive an Outback bowl bid against the Florida State Seminoles. Jaevery would lead the team in tackles with 84 for the season. The game against Florida State was a game that Jaevery's team could have restored some pride back into the program and help propel the team into spring practice as well as fall camp. They had just finished what was a trying season. The hype is to be achieved not believed or conceived. The players and coaches had a lot to play for. Having an 8-5 season was much better than a 7-6 season. Beating a talented Florida State team would have taken some of the disappointment of the season away. The game was another special event for the family and friends of Jaevery because it was in Orlando, Florida again. Jaevery was making his fourth straight trip to a bowl game in Florida. About twenty five family members and friends attended the game. Jaevery's teammates were very gracious in supplying him with tickets that they didn't use. Another reason the game was special was Jaevery was getting a chance to play against his friend Antoine Smith. Smith was the starting running back for the Seminoles who Jaevery played recreation football with and I was their coach. I talked about how good I was at assessing talent and Smith was proof of that. I was on the field running my team through some conditioning drills when I saw this stocky and compact young man walking toward the registering booth with his football cleats wrapped around his shoulders. I hollered out "hey young man come over here, I'll sign you up"! Smith came and started practicing with my team, to make a long story short, he would go on and win three state championships in high school and be the number one running back in the country his senior year in high school. I know the foundation was set with what he learned while playing under my tutelage. He says the same thing today. He is now a running back for the Atlanta Falcons in the NFL.

The starting weak side linebacker sustained a knee injury that would keep him out of the game. A top safety didn't play because of a positive drug screen. Jaevery was moved back to weakside linebacker and the other young linebacker played the middle. Jaevery and I talked about being opportunistic during the game. We talked about making plays when a play was there to be made. I reminded him of the last two bowl games he played in he had chances to make big plays and he didn't.

The game started out close in the first quarter. After a backward pass in the backfield was pick up and taken in for a touchdown, the route was on. Nothing went right offensively or defensively for Jaevery's team.

Florida State's punter kept the offense penned back on their side of the field. Play calling and execution was bad. Players looked like they couldn't wait for the game to be over. I remember seeing the starting defensive end hollering and screaming at his teammates trying to get them fired up, but to no avail. Jaevery played a pretty good game when he was inside where the action was. Playing the weak side linebacker position, sometimes it has you away from the ball. You are really another cornerback that can tackle. The defense took an overall beating, especially the secondary. The top safety being out didn't help.

After the game, Jaevery met with his family and friends. He was always greeted with love and affection after these games win or lose. When we got a chance to talk, Jaevery talked about the speed and physicality that Florida State played with. He said it reminded him of when he was in high school. Jaevery talked to me about when they met Florida State in the middle of the field before the game, some of the players didn't come and some were reluctant when they did. I told him that I noticed that sitting in the stands. You can't allow a team like Florida State to smell fear. They did and the outcome of the game was evidence of that.

A 7-6 season was now over. All the hype that the team received was all for not. If a team believed they were as good as people said they were it was Jaevery's 2008 team. The so called leaders of that team were I and me players. Meaning, I want my numbers and get me the ball. They played when they wanted to play. They didn't show up every game. The coaches didn't allow that mentality to linger around. Immediately after the Florida State lose, the head coach incorporated a zero tolerance policy concerning accountability and discipline.

THY WILL WAS DONE

While riding home from Orlando, Jaevery talked about the realization that he only had one more season to play and that same amount of time to graduate. At home during the winter break, we talked mostly about leading by example. We talked about how the mindset of the team had to change and the returning seniors would have to lead that charge. Jaevery put a lot into his strength and conditioning during that time once again. His knee would still swell up. But it didn't limit his preparation. It's funny how the 2009 anthem, theme or whatever you want to call it was (finish). Finishing strong was also a topic that I continually talked to Jaevery about. Football was a priority, but I was constantly talking to Jaevery about finishing strong academically. I would talk to him about the good choices and good decisions that he had made up to that point. I always told him how proud I was of him, but I would always make him take time to acknowledge himself and to be proud of the new territory he was about to embark on. I would tell him, don't drop your guards now. I knew it was still my job to enhance his motivation. The skull sessions were flowing from my heart. My son was about to graduate from one of the most prestigious universities in the world, not country, the world. I always looked at Jaevery being receptive to what I say as a major blessing. We never had to wrestle with each other on what I thought was right for him. He did a beautiful job allowing me to be his father. The love of Jesus Christ has to be in you to be able to do that. Some people say it's natural for a young man to rebel against the will of his father. To that I say "that's why I feel so blessed, because it did not happen to me". Jaevery will walk up to me and tell me he loves me just because. Listening to my advice was something he looked forward to. A good example of that was the bible verse from Psalm 119:97-100, which I introduced him to when he had his position change. Jaevery had verse 98 tattooed on his forearm. When he showed the tattoo to me he said, "see daddy, I'm always listening to you". He didn't need to do that, tattooing his arm wasn't necessary, I'd been convince of him listening to me for years.

Throughout the winter, we talked about closing the last chapter of his career with class, respect and honor. Jaevery left to resume classes and winter conditioning. This was the first winter conditioning that coach H. was the head strength and conditioning coach. Coach H. had been the assistant Jaevery's previous seasons. Coach H. implemented competition in many of the different phases of the workouts where there were winners and losers, which I thought was great. That type of atmosphere allows each individual to compete with a winner's mentality. When there's nothing at stake, the energy in the competition is not the same. It was during these workouts that Jaevery started telling me he thought that team was going to be special. That was his last season coming up. That was also his fourth winter conditioning session. Why the optimism after just going through a 7-6 season was my question? He stated, "Coach H. is pushing us to another level and it's making us closer. "And it's making us closer". My thoughts on that statement was coach H. understand what the DNA of a championship team is. When you are close on a team, the capacity of good things happening becomes greater. Coach H. was creating new minds in individuals. He was creating a new way of thinking with the words accountability and finish being the main focus. Hard work was also an ingredient. Like the saying goes, hard work beat talent when talent doesn't work hard. Jaevery's knee was still and issue, but he would get treatment and be right back to work the next day doing his best to lead by example.

During my nightly conversation with Jaevery, he would always talk about the effect that coach H. was having on the team. He talked about how the seniors were making an impact in their own little way. I would have Jaevery reflect back to when he was a senior in high school. His senior year in high school, he carried that team offensively and defensively. He did it with quiet leadership. It was now his time to do the same thing with his 2009 team. I would tell him leadership deals with a lot of things. You have to be early and stay late. You have to go to class, tutoring and study hall. You have to have a good report at the training table and the locker room. Consistency in all those area would be the key in getting your teammates to follow you. You can't be up and down in your approach to lead. If you are, you will get some followers, but you don't want some, you want all. I would text Jaevery things like, a leader is one who knows the way, shows the way and goes the way. I would also tell him that a leader makes his own path and leave a trail for others to follow. Our nightly conversations, which we were still having, consisted of encouraging words. From a father's perspective, I could see the light at the end of the tunnel. Concerning football, Jaevery was the leading tackler returning and academically he was on pace to graduate from one of the most prestigious universities in the world, not the country, but the world. I was witnessing the manifestation of the prayers that I had been praying for years. I knew the hand of God was on Jaevery's life and God's will for Jaevery's life would be done. The job I had was to interrupt corrupt conversation. Jaevery had to always feel like a winner, that was my job. Whatever he heard from his coaches, teammates or peers that was negative I was the person that had to rebuke that and let him know that he was walking in God's will for his life. I would tell Jaevery that affirmation, conformation and validation from man is like a house built on sand, when the storm comes, the house washes away. I talked to him about the things he had already gone through and now was the time to focus on having a wonderful senior season.

Spring practice 2009 was upon Jaevery's team. With Jaevery being the only linebacker that got significant playing time in '08 that position and the defensive line were positions that the coaches needed to see improvement in. The secondary was solid with the corners and safeties being all returning players. The coaches decided to move Jaevery back to weak side linebacker in an effort to get the other young linebacker on the field. From a father's perspective, I didn't really like that move. Although, Jaevery was a good tackler in space, the weak side linebacker position takes you out of almost half of the defensive plays or more during a game.

From A Father's Perspective (On His Own)

You have the most physical player on your team always running to the play when the play is over. Jaevery didn't complain about the move, he embraced it. It was lemonade time again. During these practices Jaevery would be at the weak side, the young linebacker in the middle and B.S. at the strong side. All the linebackers were good friends, but Jaevery and B. S. became close. Jaevery would visit B.S. home in Minnesota when the team had off days. Jaevery was happy to see B.S. finally getting his opportunity to play. The team was coming together. The coaches got a chance to look at a lot of different people at different position. Z. B. got most of the carries at running back because J. C. had knee problems. The offensive line was working new players in trying to find continuity. D. S., S. T. and C. P. were battling for the quarterback position. I arrived in that Midwest City for the last week of practices and I watched the spring game. Jaevery was his usual self in those last practices leading up to the game. He would have a big hit, a tackle for loss or an interception in each practice. He was making plays all over the field. But, the thing about it was the plays were being made down the field. If Jaevery was in the middle those plays would have went for less yards. After one of the practices, the head coach approached me like he had before and talked to me about Jaevery's progress. He said the usual, Jaevery was playing well and he was looking good. He then said something to me that took me aback. The head coach stated to me that he was scared for Jaevery because Jaevery was hanging with S. C. S. C. had some off the field incidents that kept him off the team at various times. S. C. and Jaevery also hung out together off the field. That friendship had been going on since their freshman year. Jaevery hadn't done anything to warrant that type of concern. Why would he wait until his senior year to do something to alter his goal? Not to mention I was in his ear every night. Again, I just listened to the head coach. Jaevery was not a follower. S.C. or no one else on that team could influence Jaevery to do anything. I never mentioned that conversation between the head coach and I to Jaevery. B. S. was also having an impressive spring. He was supposed to be battling M.T. for the strong side linebacker position. With M. T. being out with an injury, B. S. took advantage of all the reps he got and performed well. The game drew a nice crowd for the second year in a row. The fans were eager to see what this group would look like. The head coach would hold true to his accountability theme when he benched the starting defensive end for being a couple minutes late to a meeting the night before the spring game.

The game was able to show the fans and the naysayers that the team had a chance to bounce back from the "don't believe the hype 7-6 season". The quarterback position was up for grabs, but Z.B., J.C.and the receivers looked good. The defense also played well. D. S. helped the defense out by throwing an interception right to linebacker for a pick six. Jaevery had about nine or ten tackles, but, again, most of them were beyond the line of scrimmage. During the spring game the coaches usually let the so called star players play only a half or less with the intent on preventing injuries. Jaevery ended up playing the entire game. From a father's perspective, I was thinking give Jaevery a rest, what else do he have to prove? Besides, he was playing on a knee that continued to swell. I just knew the coaches would sit Jaevery after the half. I was burning inside watching him play the whole second half. You had to know Jaevery's mannerisms to see that he was running and favoring his knee. He practiced all spring like that also. I'm thinking give the poor kid a break.

After the game I took pictures of Jaevery signing autographs. I took as many pictures as I could, knowing this would be the last spring I would watch Jaevery at the stadium. I couldn't help but think about how he suppressed the pain he was feeling as he accommodated every boy; girl and adult who ask him to sign something or take a picture with them. After about fifteen minutes of me taking pictures, Jaevery and I walked to the locker room. I asked Jaevery how did his knee feel and he said," Ah, man I couldn't wait until the game was over." Jaevery told me he thought the coaches were going to take him out the game at the half. I asked him why did the coaches keep him in the game and he said he didn't know. I let him know that he looked good and how I wished he was playing in the middle. I went to the meet and greet where Jaevery would later join me. The head coach and the defensive coordinator made their rounds and talked to me about Jaevery playing a good game and for Jaevery to continue to show leadership by going to class and doing all the little things. My thoughts were on why was one of your best players playing in the second half when he already had a knee the size of a grapefruit. I held my peace and just went along with their conversation. After the meet and greet was over, Jaevery went for treatment and I went to get him three bags of ice to take to his apartment so that he could continue to treat his knee throughout the night.

From A Father's Perspective (On His Own)

With the spring game now over, the focus for Jaevery now was fulfilling his dream. He had one more season to play and one more semester of academics. The will of God was manifesting itself concerning Jaevery's life for that season. Jaevery's job was to stay in God's will. I would continue to remind him that the end was near. I would tell him that good choices and good decision are more important now than they ever were. I often said to him that there are no mistakes allowed. From a father's perspective, I went back to when Jaevery first told me he wanted to play football, to him and I working out with my brother and his sons, to Jaevery being the best defensive player on the rec league team, to M.V.P. in high school, to crying because his position was changed, to becoming a starter, to saying to me how the head coach and the defensive coordinatior don't know how to talk to people, dealing with death in the family, his home burning, injuries, women, being 1500 miles away from home, winters in the Midwest, the ups and downs of college football and academics. The fact that he overcame all those things and more solidified to me that God's will was being done in Jaevery's life. He was happy, I was happy and his mother was happy. When mom is happy, everything is alright.

Jaevery being home for the summer is a beautiful thing. His mother just loved him being around and she liked to cook for him. Their interaction was special to see. I would often hear Jaevery tell his mom that he loved her and he would give her kisses on her cheek spontaneously. This was his last summer as a college football player and he wanted it to be special. He worked out at the L.A. Fitness and did some running on the beach in the morning. He would do his position drills in the evening with some of his friends that also played college football. Our skull sessions were still being done with the focus on finishing strong. I would tell Jaevery that God was doing his part and all he had to do was to stay in the will. Playing college football and graduating from a prestigious university in the Big Ten was Jaevery's dream and he was living it. My dream was to see it and I was witnessing it first hand up close and in person. We also talked about what it was that he wanted to bring to the team when he went back for summer conditioning. Jaevery talked about toughness and teaching the younger players what it meant to be on the team. He said he wanted to take the young linebackers like M. T. and C. B. under his wings so that they could be effective early and help the team. I told him that I remember when that was him and when I told him to absorb all he could because he was going to have to share what he learned with the young talent that was coming in. That time had come and he was about to get that opportunity to do so. Night in and night out we would rehash conversations pertaining to finishing his senior season strong and staying in God's will for his life.

Jaevery left for summer conditioning and summer classes for 2009. I was still calling every night before I went to bed. He would tell me how competitive coach H. was making the workouts and how much stronger he and his teammates were getting. Jaevery would reiterate how close the team was becoming and he would talk about how players were making plays when they would play seven on seven. I would tell him to look at that time in the summer as preparation time to get his mind and body right for the upcoming season. He agreed that that was what that time was for and he wasn't going to waste one minute of it. Throughout the summer I would here from Jaevery about how he felt that team was going to surprise people. He would say, "Daddy, I just have a feeling." Based on the season that Jaevery had in 2008 some scouts had him between a fifth and seventh round pick in the 2010 NFL Draft. No doubt about it, Jaevery had NFL aspirations. A good gauge of how the coaches were thinking about who would be the face of the team was who made the trip to The Big Ten Kick-off Luncheon in July. The coaches would pick three people to take to Chicago for two or three days to interact with the media. I was extremely proud when it was announced that Jaevery was chosen as one of the representatives along with O'B. S. and G. G. Being one of the best of thirty-three Big Ten players was a good pre-season reward. Jaevery was honored that the coaches chose him to represent the his team. I can recall being proud myself. I kept up with that particular event every year. Jaevery being chosen made me think that the coaches had plans for Jaevery that would get the best out of his talent. In some of the interviews that the head coach did, he mentioned that all three players had NFL potential. Coaches knew the desire of those three young men was the NFL. The thing they had to do now was to find a way to exploit their talent in their offensive and defensive system. Based on what had happened the season before, those three players would play a key role in the team's success. Jaevery had a beautiful time while in Chicago. He was named best dressed by one of the reporters. I can remember talking to him one night and him telling me that downtown Chicago was a beautiful thing along with making friends with the other players.

From A Father's Perspective (On His Own)

    Fall camp 2009, the last time around. Camp wasn't a week old and the head coach would kick S. C. and A. P. off the team indefinitely. The safety position was one of the strongest positions on the defense and now it was becoming a question mark because of the unknown back-ups. C. M. and J. V. would start, but the depth was weak. I could imagine how Coach K. C. and Coach R. Mc. felt during that time. No reason was given for S. C. and A. P. being kicked off the team. Jaevery, S. C. and A. P. were best friends with each other. Jaevery was hurting for his teammates. When I ask him what happened, he had no clue. Day after day went by without a word concerning if S. C. and A. P. would be reinstated. To this day one can only speculate what happened and why the head coach chose to handle the incident the way that he did. From a father's perspective, if the incident wasn't bad enough to be made public, allow those young men to return to the team. Keeping all the information private should have meant that the head coach was going to deal with the matter in house. Two fifth year senior safeties that played a tremendous amount of football were now kicked off the team. That incident reminded me of the incident with the pass rush extraordinaire. Something that could have been taken care of in house was taken to the extreme. Why not a game or two suspension? If that one incident made the head coach that fed up with S. C. and A. P. what else did they do before that hellacious act. Again, these are two fifth year senior safeties with big time game experience. The back in of your defense is where you want that type of experience. No way do S. C. and A. O. not play for me. Whatever they did the conversation that I would have had with them and letting them remain on the team would have been a moment that they would have never forgotten. Those two young men knowing that they had been given a second chance or sixth chance would have been indebted to the head coach for life. How do you think the head coach would have felt to have those same young men come to him later in life and say coach if it wasn't for you given me a another opportunity to rectify my wrong, I would have never known how my senior season would have turned out. I'm forever grateful. The same thing could have happen with the pass rush extraordinaire. That didn't happen because of the head coach's iron hand. I understand disciplining to try and make a statement, but at what cost. It's easy to kick players off the team if they violate one of the team rules, but what does it say about a coach that says I'm going to stick with that young man. He knows he was wrong and I know he was wrong, but I told his parents when I recruited him I would be there for him through the good and the bad. That was a bad time, but it couldn't have been that bad if it wasn't made public. You dealt with the situation anyway enduring speculation from all. Handle the situation in house and no one knows that anything happened.

This was Jaevery's last camp and my wife and I tried to make it a special and memorable one for Jaevery as we could. My wife cooked breakfast for Jaevery and his roommate D. M. as many days as she could. We were there for a total of twenty four days. I watched the last two weeks of camp and the first two games of the season. During camp, Jaevery was his usual self concerning making plays and standing out on defense. I saw a player that was hard to block, physical and always around the ball. On third down plays, Jaevery was lining up at rush end and giving those right tackles a fit. Jaevery would have those types of practices during the morning and evening practices. Based on how Jaevery was being used during fall camp, I knew he would have a good season. The annual Family Day came around and Jaevery, O'B. A. and G. G. sat with the head coach to sign autographs. They signed shirts, hats, card, posters you name it they were signing it. I may have taken at least one hundred and fifty pictures during the two or three hours that the event lasted. I ran into A. P.'s father and we talked. He didn't dispose any information about why A. P. was kicked off the team only stating that lawyers were handling the situation. We were standing by the table where the head coach, Jaevery, O'B. S. and G. G. were sitting. Mr. P. gave the head coach a stare down that said if me and you were in an alley only I would come out of that alley. Mr. P. was ticked off and from a father's perspective, rightfully so. The head coach must have known that there might be an issue because one of the city's finest (police) was standing by his side. Mr. P. never said anything to me about harming the head coach or anything like that, he just used what he had and that was a menacing look.

Jaevery, O'B.S. and G. G. sitting with the head coach was becoming a theme. They were the same three players chosen to represent his team at The Big Ten Kickoff Luncheon. Add another player to that group and you have your four captains for the 2009 season was my thinking. I guess that's what I get for thinking. The night before the captains were picked, the head coach asked Jaevery to stand up and address the team. Jaevery talked about persevering through injuries, position changes, waiting his turn to play, keeping his nose clean and just being an overall program guy. Jaevery talked about not worrying about stats and doing whatever the coaches needed him to do for the team he did it. Camp was drawing to an end and the captains had to be picked. The next practice was on a Wednesday and classes had started that day or were starting the next day. What I do know was State Street would be full of Jaevery's teammates until the wee hours of the morning. With about two weeks left in camp, Jaevery asked me and his mother if we would buy him a ticket to see his favorite rap artist Lil' Wayne. My question to Jaevery was is there any curfew because camp would be still going on. Jaevery assured me that there was no curfew and the ticket was bought. Again, the wife and I are thinking let's do something nice for him, he's working hard and doing everything we've asked him to do. The Bible says, hold no good thing from those who walk uprightly. In my wife eyes and my eyes Jaevery was doing that. Jaevery posted that he was going to the concert which was approximately fifty five minutes away in another Midwest City on his twitter page. The head coach saw that Jaevery had posted that on his twitter page and when practice was over in front of trainers, managers, the team and everybody else that is usually there when the team circle up after practice, he cursed Jaevery using f-bombs and asked him how could he stand in front of the team the night before and then go to a concert the next night. He would go on to call Jaevery a hypocrite. I was standing on the sideline and heard every word the head coach said. God is good all the time. The head coach didn't know how bad I wanted to let him know that cursing my son like that wasn't necessary. The point could have been made in a different way. I greeted Jaevery and said you are not going to the concert huh? He stated, I guess not. Jaevery and I went to dinner and I told him that the defensive coordinator was going to call him to see where he was. I said that to Jaevery because I knew that was how the defensive coordinator was. Right after I said that Jaevery's phone rang and it was the defensive coordinator I hollered, "he's right here with me coach, were eating dinner." I could have asked Jaevery to let me speak to him and explain why I bought the ticket, but I chose not to. Jaevery and the defensive coordinator talked awhile then he hung up the phone. The defensive coordinator made the statement to Jaevery that going to that concert could affect his family. He was thinking if Jaevery were to get in trouble he would have to find someone else to play Jaevery's position. You had half of the team on State Street until the wee hours in the morning, but Jaevery couldn't stay out until 11 or 12am. He was going to use my rental car and when he returned I was going to take him home. All the head coach and defensive coordinator could see was Jaevery being in a car with A.P. and S.C. doing whatever their minds would allow them to think and getting caught by the police. For the defensive coordinator to say that Jaevery going to that concert would affect his family that had to be his thoughts. What made it so bad was, S.C. and A.P. wasn't who Jaevery was going with. Some Badgers did go to that concert, but Jaevery wasn't one of them.

When the captains were announced the next day, Jaevery wasn't one of them neither. Jaevery McFadden from Riviera Beach, Florida, young man who persevered through the ups and downs of college football, lead the team in tackles the previous year, who thought he was doing everything right was looked over as a captain. Jaevery had a good report with all the players on the team. You would think it was a rap that he would be named a captain. I think the head coach held the fact that Jaevery wanted to go to that concert against him and chose who he wanted to be a captain. Plus the young men that were chosen were players that the head coach liked to tell stories about. How C.M. being from the Midwest, but he went to Western Michigan out of high school and later transferred and earned a scholarship. C.M. transferred in as a wide receiver and was switched to safety. Not to mention his family was season ticket holders since he was a kid. With all due respect to M. T., he must have been a heck of a teammate in the locker room and off the field. G.G. and O'B. S. was obvious picks. I thought Jaevery would be also. It is said that the players pick the captains, yeah right! J.C. was a captain his junior year and was not voted a captain his senior year with the same players returning. He didn't lose popularity with his teammates; he lost popularity with the coaches. Jaevery told me when J.C.'s name was not called to be a captain his senior year I should have saw his face. Jaevery said J.C. was overwhelmingly surprised. When I found out that next morning that Jaevery didn't make captain, I called him and asked him was he alright. The answer that I got from him surprised me, but after I thought about the answer that he gave me it was Jaevery at his best. Jaevery's answer to me was, "no sweat off my back". Jaevery went on to say that he would have been honored to be a captain, but he wasn't going to dwell on the fact that he wasn't chosen.

From A Father's Perspective (On His Own)

I can remember being proud of the way Jaevery talked to me about that situation. Jaevery being a captain may have meant more to me than it did to him. I wasn't wrong for wanting or even thinking that Jaevery would be named a captain. If two captains are picked from the offense and the defense with the players returning Jaevery was a lock was my thought and wish. Again, from a father's perspective, I think the head coach made the decision that no matter if Jaevery was voted captain he was going to veto the player's decision.

Fall camp 2009 was different from all the previous camps. Jaevery didn't have to prove anything. He wasn't trying to win a position or trying to compete for playing time. On the defense he was quote unquote the man and he proved that every practice. B. S. also had a good camp. He and M. T. were competing for the starting strong side linebacker position. M. T. was coming off and injury that kept him from practicing a lot in camp. M.T. may have practice about a week with the first team and the coaches ended up starting him instead of B.S. They moved B.S. to middle linebacker stating that he was now competing with the young linebacker for playing time. M.T. was given that starting position, he didn't earn it. To justify what they did, they said they needed depth at the middle linebacker position and B.S. provided that. I remember talking to B.S.'s father at the first game of the season about the move and he was very humble about it. He took the high road and didn't say anything negative about the coaches and their decisions. But, I did say that I thought B.S. should be starting.

The games came quickly. S. T. won the quarterback job over D. S. and C. P. S.T.'s play kind of reminded me of Jaevery and how he became a starter. Watching S.T. play the first two games led me to believe that the Badgers were going to have a chance to win every game that they played. I was able to see why Jaevery was so optimistic about the season. I also thought about why S.T. didn't start ahead of A.E. and D. S. the year before. The way S. T. played showed that all he needed was an early opportunity to play. The coaches dropped the ball on that evaluation. If a sophomore is neck to neck in overall talent with a fifth year senior and a fourth year junior who haven't played much then that sophomore should be given an opportunity to start or at least play a lot. Neither scenario happened for S.T. The coaches would have you to think that all of a sudden the lights turned on and S. T. figured everything out. Yeah, right. The truth of the matter was if that kid would have played the year before he would have played the same way he played his junior and senior year. Jaevery became a starter the same way. The ability to start was shown early, but the coaches were in love with other players.

What Jaevery talked to me about during the winter, spring and fall I was witnessed in person the first two games. The offense was very diverse. They could run for one hundred yards or pass for one hundred yard. They also had the capacity to do both in the same game. The defense displayed toughness and a bend but don't break attitude. I could recall saying to my wife after the fifth game of the season that the Badgers had a chance to go to the Rose Bowl. My reasoning for that statement was because the Badgers had a quarterback and a stellar defense. O'B. S. was leading the defense making big plays behind the line of scrimmage and pressuring the quarterback. Jaevery's play was consistent although he did have three personal foul penalties in the first three games. I wasn't happy with the way Jaevery was being used. I felt that he was too far away from the action. He may as well have been playing cornerback. The middle of the field is where Jaevery should have been. I know coaches want to get different players on the field, but at whose sacrifice. Jaevery played the middle with one hand the year before. His senior season was the year for him to run sideline to sideline and to be put in position to make plays from the edge. I saw that during camp, but when the game came around C. B. was on the edge and Jaevery, the toughest player on the team, was playing cornerback (really weak side linebacker, but you get the picture). All due respect to C.B. but those opportunities should have been Jaevery's, he was the fifth year senior with NFL aspiration. There is no doubt you do what you need to do to win the games, but you also put your best players in position to be seen and graded for the next level.

As the season went on the Jaevery's team suffered a disappointed loss to the Ohio State Buckeyes. The defense dominate the Buckcyes the whole first half until about the last couple of minutes. Terrel Pryor broke containment on one play, there was a play where the head coach could have challenged a catch by the Buckeyes tight end, but he didn't and that play kept the drive going. The Buckeyes scored a play or two later on a pass play taking the momentum into the locker room. Players are going to make mistakes, but for the coaches not to see that the ball hit the ground before that tight end caught that ball is inexcusable. The Buckeyes also scored three touchdowns on two interception returns for touchdowns and a kick-off return for a touchdown. The defense ended up playing a big time game, but was not able to overcome the three scores that they weren't on the field for. The offense held the ball for forty-three minutes and the Badgers still lost. Jaevery played with a sore ankle in that game that he sustained a week before in the game against Minnesota. Mind you he was still getting treatment on his knee.

On a daily bases during the week at approximately 11:30 am ct Jaevery would meet with the defensive coordinator. Their meeting would consist of watching film and disgusting that day's practice expectations. You would think that all that time with someone would bring you to a place where you could communicate with them on and off the field in a respectful manner. A fifth year senior and a defensive coordinator that have been in the same program for four years should have a report where they could respectfully disagree. If Jaevery made a mistake in practice the defensive coordinator would still curse at him as though he never knew him, but the next day Jaevery would be right back in his office watching film. You would think after watching all that film Jaevery would be able to move away from tendencies if he thought he saw something in the formation. Film watching is supposed to make you better at your craft. I didn't see that in Jaevery. He was always hesitant or waiting for someone to come and block him. Sometime Jaevery looked like a robot playing out there afraid to make a mistake. His instincts were better than that. Recognizing run or pass is not that hard. I asked Jaevery about the relationship he and the defensive coordinator had and he said," It is what it is daddy", "I don't let what he say affect me. With the right conversation coaches has the capacity to free a player up and let him play. It's like a good basketball player who is needed to score for the team, but he's worried about missing shots and making mistakes. If that coach tell that player I've got you're back, your scoring is needed in order for this team to be successful and not to worry about misses or mistakes then that player will play better and become the player that he knows he is. I really felt like that was all Jaevery needed, but instead he would get cursed out and even taken out of some defensive packages. The right words are the things that moved the best people into their respective destinies. Words are not just noise or sounds they are spirits. I've lived this. Jaevery was able to do what he did because of the words that I and his mother spoke over his life. Other forces tried to hinder the process directly or indirectly, but the words were already spoken.

At the halfway point the Jaevery's team were 5-1 and heading into a big game against Iowa. I usually ask Jaevery if he is in on all the defensive packages but I didn't this time. During the first third down situation I notice Jaevery jogging off the field. I was sitting on my couch livid. I'm thinking there is no way that Jaevery should be coming off the field at any time on that defense unless he is hurt and can't go. C. B., B. S. and M.T. were on the field on third down. What NFL scout or G. M. is going to give a second thought to a senior linebacker that can't be on the field on third down. The defensive coordinator was messing with Jaevery's family now. This is the same person that meets with you every day at 11:30a.m. and watch film of the opposing team. Jaevery made a quote unquote name for himself by coming on the field on third down during the 2007 season as a redshirt sophomore and now he's being taken off the field as a fifth year senior. Watching that was unbelievable. If M. T. doesn't get hurt, Jaevery probably would have been running off the field on the third down the rest of the season. In this life you have to have faith that things would work out. M.T.'s injury solidified that Jaevery would be in on third down like he should have been anyway for the rest of the season. The defensive coordinator had no other choice or option, but to play Jaevery. God's will was done. Jaevery was being disrespected by being pulled off the field on the third down. Jaevery is not the type of kid that's going to give the coaches a hard time about a decision like that and the coaches knew that. I'm not saying God caused M. T. to get hurt, but I knew something had to happen so that Jaevery could be on the field every defensive snap. Week in and week out Jaevery played okay. He never had that one stamp game like I saw him dominate in high school. In the game against Purdue he came close to that. He not only made plays in the run game, but he was alignment and assignment strong in the passing game. Jaevery did a good job rerouting the Purdue receivers causing the quarterback to hold on to the ball longer. The front four made a lot of plays due to Jaevery's effort on passing downs. I was at the stadium for that game. The Friday after the team walk through, the defensive coordinator, who always came and spoke to me before or after practice, I felt intentionally avoided talking to me. Just my feelings and from a father's perspective. The way Jaevery was treated by being benched on third down he knew it was wrong. I felt he knew Jaevery and I talked about it and he couldn't, no not couldn't but, he wouldn't face me. I'm thinking he probably thought I had words for him. He did wave at me when I saw him at the arc where the team get off the bus and walk through. I was standing where he had to see me and he acknowledged me. You can feel when a person knows that they wronged you or one of yours and I felt that from the defensive coordinator. After that game Jaevery and I met at the indoor practice facility. We talked to players and parents for about thirty to forty minutes then we walked to the rental car I had. As we got close to the rental car I started to reach into my pockets for the keys. I checked all my pockets and the keys were not there. I had on a leather jacket and a hoody because it was Wisconsin cold that Saturday. Jaevery asked me did I check the pockets on my hoody and I answered him "yes I did". We continued to walk to the car. When we got to the car I was hoping that the keys were in the ignition because if they were there the door would be unlocked. No such luck was to be had, the keys weren't there. I told Jaevery that I was going to go and back track the route I took when I met the team at the arc. I walked approximately fifty yards until the Holy Spirit directed me to turn around and go back. I was then told by the Holy Spirit to turn right and stop. When I stopped the Holy Spirit said look down by your right foot. When I looked down by my right foot, the keys were right by my right shoe. I quickly called Jaevery who was still standing behind the car. Jaevery came and I told him to look down by my right foot. Jaevery reached down and picked the keys up. He couldn't believe what he saw. I told Jaevery that things happen in life so that God can show himself strong in your life. Jaevery had to witness something like this for himself. The keys had fallen out of my pocket as soon as I got out of the car. When I closed the car door, I took off running trying to make sure that I caught Jaevery coming through the arc. The keys were nestled down in some beautiful yellow, red, rust, green and brown colored leaves. Without the help of the Holy Spirit I would not have found those keys. The way they were nestled in those leaves you couldn't just see them. I saw them because I was told by The Holy Spirit to look there.

With four games left to play Jaevery's play was acceptable I guess. As his father I knew he could do better. Jaevery's mother and I along with other family members prepared to attend Parents Day. Parents Day is when the seniors get to run to the forty-five yard line where their family members are standing waiting for them. This was a special event for me. When

Jaevery was a true freshman I was at the Parents Day game. I watched the festivities and how everyone was so proud of their sons. I made a deal with God that night. I told God that if he allowed me to see Jaevery reached that moment in his career, I would get on my knees in front of all the people in the stadium and raise my hands to the sky giving him praise. I couldn't wait until the day of the game. I was anxious to honor my deal with God. The day of the game was finally here. Jaevery's team would play The University of Michigan, who they owed some revenge from the year before. My wife and I, two of Jaevery's uncles, two of his aunts, a friend of the family and my nephew Jeremy flew into that Midwest City the Friday before the game. Jaevery playing in his last game at Camp Randell was a beautiful thing. My wife, uncle Lump, Jeremy and myself had a nice breakfast with the other parents in the inside facility. We then were escorted on the field. It was electric down there. The announcer begins to call out the names and he finally got to Jaevery. Jaevery was hyped as usual. He was yelling and waving to the crowd. As he started toward us I fell to my knees and honored God like I said I would. I saw my wife hug Jaevery and begin to cry. She didn't want to let him go. I got up off my knees and I hugged Jaevery after my brother in law and nephew did. I was a proud father who was thankful that God honored me in the deal I made with him. I was happy that God kept angels around Jaevery every day for four and a half years without him being seriously hurt or in any trouble. Jaevery traveled all the time while he was in that Midwest City. He would go to Minnesota, Tennessee, New York, Atlanta, Detroit and South Beach all the time. Not to mention when he went out in that Midwest City. I know that God had angels watching over Jaevery all the time. Young men were dying every day within the five years that Jaevery was in that Midwest City. At the University of Miami and the University of Conneticut to name a few. God watching over Jaevery as he traveled from city to city, slept in his apartment and all the other little things were what I was thankful for. The enemy didn't win, thank you Jesus.

In the game Jaevery played well. He suffered an ankle sprain that kind of slowed him up on making more plays, but there was no way he was coming off the field in his last game at home in front of 84,000 people. After the game we all had a beautiful dinner and talked about the experience. I was still flowing on cloud nine on the deal me and God made. Jaevery's team played Northwestern the following week and suffered a disappointing defeat. J. C. fumbled the ball as the offense was driving for a game winning field goal. That lost left the Badgers at 8-3. The next game was at Hawaii. The team was trying to finish the regular season on a winning note. A record of 9-3 is much better than 8-4. The team took a trip to Pearl Harbor and they spent some time on the beach. Sometimes the tendency can be to enjoy Hawaii and its splendor rather than to play the game. Jaevery's team played well in all phases and dealt Hawaii a convincing lost. Jaevery's team finished the regular season 9-3 and answered the critics concerning their ability to bounce back from a 7-6 season the year before.

What was left for Jaevery as a student athlete was to graduate and to play his last college football game. The game was a bowl game against the University of Miami. The team prepared for the bowl game with the thoughts of utilizing that game to propel them into the 2010 season. This was a good Miami team that Jaevery's team was playing. They were ranked 14 in the country at the time. But, first things first. There was a graduation to go to. Jaevery Jamille McFadden was about to graduate from one of the top universities in the world. During the chancellor's speech she stated that the university that Jaevery graduated from was one of the top 20 universities in the world. My wife, my seventy-seven years old mother, two of my sisters, my wife's sister and my nephew Jeremy accompanied me at the graduation. While sitting in the basketball arena where the commencement took place, I took about ten minutes to take in the blessing that was about to take place. A young black male from Riviera Beach, Florida was about to graduate from a predominately and prestigiously white university. The chancellor started to call names and she was stating that individuals were from four generations of graduates from the university. I have an associate of arts degree from a junior college here in Florida in Journalism and Communications. My son was getting ready to walk across the stage with a Bachelor of Arts degree in Sociology. God's will was done. When Jaevery walked across that stage I was ecstatic. The dream was fulfilled. The little boy with the dream to play college football and get a college degree had accomplished his dream and I was able to come along for the ride. God is so good! We showered Jaevery with love and adoration for the rest of the day and night. You could see the glow on his face and the feeling of accomplishment exuding from him. He had done what he sat out to do and he could now be an example to others. He could now speak to young people on adversity, faith, hope, perseverance and personal fortitude and they would be smart to listen because he endured it all and reaped the benefits.

The next thing on the agenda of accomplishments was to beat Miami. This game had some personal significant for Jaevery and me. I've always been a Miami fan. I prayed every night for the four years that Jaevery was in high school that Miami would recruit Jaevery. That didn't happen and we wanted to make them pay for that. Jaevery was a first team all-state player that wasn't recruited by any of the top state universities. This was an opportunity to show Miami what they could have had. This was also another chance for the family to see Jaevery play for the last time in Florida. The family made its way to Orlando for the Champs Sports Bowl. The game was full of excitement. Jaevery played a very good game. Jaevery's team defense was good all game. They pressured the quarterback and made key stops on third down. Jaevery had several third down stops. The game ended with Jaevery's team winning 20-14. Jaevery was elated after the game. Winning the last game of his college career against the team he grew up wanting to play for. God's will was done. The next morning as we drove from Orlando to our home in Riviera Beach, Jaevery received text message after text message from teammates stating how much they were going to miss him and the influence that he made on their lives. He was teary eyed in the back seat. He mentioned J. C., B. S., A. H., P. M., L. K. and O'B. S. As my brother in law drove down the turnpike it gave me a chance to reflect on the journey. I thought about God and how this was what he wanted to happen in our lives. Before the foundation of the world was framed God ordained these beautiful times in our lives and the gates of hell couldn't prevail against us. Jesus is real. Without Him none of this would have been possible, but with Him it happened. Philippians 4:13 says, I can do all things through Christ which strengthened me. It docsn't say some things it says all things. To live every second, minute, hour, day, month, and year with the hope and the faith that my son's dream would manifest itself was again, also my dream that came true.

Now that Jaevery had graduated and his last game was over his mind shifted to the NFL and his chance of being drafted. Some of the scouting services had Jaevery going in the seventh round or being a preferred free agent or just a free agent. You would think that the head coach or his position coach would try to have a hand in helping you. I remember the head coach telling me he might be able to get Jaevery in one of the lesser known games for seniors to showcase their talents. That never happened. I don't even know if the head coach tried. I never asked either. Some things you just do. You know this kid have NFL aspirations so you do everything in your power to try to help him. It shouldn't have been a hard sell. Good kid, good teammate, no arrests, very coachable give him a chance and you want regret it was all that needed to be said. Jaevery's play wasn't eye-popping but he was consistent. He led the team in tackles from the middle linebacker position and the weak side linebacker position at a Big Ten university on bad knees and with one hand. Jaevery wasn't invited to any senior all- star game or the NFL Combine. He had to wait and perform at his team's Pro Day. From after the bowl game until the first week of March Jaevery trained every day except Sunday to get ready for the Pro Day. Pro Day arrived with Jaevery being interviewed by the Jacksonville Jaguars that morning. I met Jaevery at his team's inside practice facility after his interview was over. He stated the interview went well. He talked about how the Jaguars management said they liked him. As I made my way into the practice facility the head coach was coming in my direction. We shook hands and he said Jacksonville said they like him. Then he said it only take one team to like you. The one thing I regret not doing was not asking the head coach this question. What did you say about Jaevery to any team? I would have like to have known if he was emphatic when he talked about Jaevery or nonchalant. Because it does matter. That scout is going to know whether to waste his time or not based on the approach and delivery of the head coach. I wish I had asked that question. I know the defensive coordinator didn't say anything to anybody because he didn't speak to me. I saw him across the field and I know he saw me. Again, it's just one of those things when you know you haven't done the right thing and you can't face that person.

    Inside the practice facility Jaevery and his teammates warmed up to prepare for their position drills. Whoever coordinated the drills had the participant do all the agility drills first and the bench press last. How are you going to do that at your best when you are gassed from the agility drills? Jaevery bench pressed 225 pounds twenty times; if they would have done it first he probably could have done four or five more. Jaevery's forty time wasn't impressive at 4.78. He vertical jumped 35inches and standing broad jumped 10feet 2 inches. All his other agility and position drills were in the same range as all the other linebackers in the draft.

The draft came and went without Jaevery being drafted. He didn't get picked up as a preferred free agent or even a free agent. He ended up being called by the Washington Redskins and went to their minicamp. No luck. He went to the Minnesota Vikings minicamp and again no luck. The Miami Dolphins called him and invited him to come in for a workout, no luck. Jaevery's agents tried to get him in the Canadian League and the United Football League, but for Jaevery it was the NFL or nothing.

Jaevery took solace in watching his former teammates on the 2010 team win the Big Ten Championship and go to the Rose Bowl. The win against Miami in the Champs Sports Bowl set the tone for the 11-1 regular season the team had. After that Miami game the head coach told the seniors of the 2009 team that if the 2010 team wins the Big Ten Championship and go to the Rose Bowl, a lot of it would have to do with the president and standard that was played with from those 2009 seniors. The head coach went on to say that he would get the seniors of the 2009 team tickets for the Rose Bowl and they would also get a Big Ten Championship ring. Well when it came time for the head coach to honor his words he reneged. He gave the excuse that it was some kind of NCAA rules violation. Coaches always want the players to keep their words, but the coaches don't practice what they preach or teach. Jaevery didn't sweat the head coach's decision or take it as a disappointment; he was use to the rejection. Jaevery was in that Midwest City for the Ohio State game and tried to get on the sideline for the Ohio State game, but was told only the players that were in the NFL could be on the sideline. He watched the game in the stands and enjoyed it more. He said it gave him a chance to talk to some of the fans. He even signed some autographs. So it all worked out for his good. Status is something else when you have it. But, when it's gone who are you. You are the head coach now, what happens when you are a defensive coordinator again? That's why nice is always good.

THE MAN BEHIND THE PERSPECTIVE

I've been a sports fan all my life. Never over the top about any team but, I loved the early Miami Hurricanes and the Hurricane teams up to the years Jaevery was in high school. Swagger and mindset can grow on you, but when you just have it, you can't be stopped. Swagger dripped off me and in competition I had the mindset of a Japanese warrior. Jaevery Jamille McFadden slept in the house with a champion every night. I wasn't able to feed my family of four brothers, four sisters, mother and father with my talent and I tried to smoke marijuana, drink and snort that feeling of not accomplishing that away. I graduated out of high school in 1980. I was one of the best defensive backs in the state of Florida. I was like a cross between Ronnie Lott and Ken Eeasley. I was also a very good basketball player. From the age of 19 to 23 years old I not only thought I was the best basketball player in the world, I knew I was. I talked about this a little in the first chapter of the book. How lengendary coach Bo Schembechler came back to my banquet and recruited me after my friend Anthony A.C. Carter's breakout freshman year. I had that type of talent. I could run and jump with the best of them. As a sophomore in high school I was able to touch the top of the square on the backboard. Not going to a major university right out of high school really got me down. The talent was there, I needed to get to a place where I could showcase it. It also didn't help that a young man that was a sophomore on the basketball team when I was a senior got a basketball scharlorship to Michigan after he graduated and a young man that was a freshman when I was a senior got a football scholarship after he graduated. Another friend of mine went on to the University of Illinois to play basketball. His name is Derek Harper. Harper played 16 years in the NBA. The teams he played for was the Dallas Mavericks, Los Angeles Lakers, New York Knicks and the Orlando Magic. Harper came out of the Illinois after his junior season which would have been 1983. He was taken number nine overall in the first round by the Dallas Mavericks. He was probably 21 or 22 years old at the time. We continued to play against each other in the summer and I always played well against him and many times my team beat his team and it was due to my play. Later after he had been in the league for about three or four years he told me "Mac I've checked Mitch Richmond and I've checked Michael Jordan, you should be in the NBA". Mitch Richmond was a former all-star MVP and you know who Michael Jordan is, you get my drift. I'm writing all this because the man behind the perspective learned just as much from what didn't happen to what did happen. Smoking marijuana, snorting cocaine and drinking for approximately seventeen years was something I did. Why I did it so long was to drown sorrow and to try to block the pain of not getting it done. Like I said earlier I thought I was the best basketball player in the world and here I am at a junior college. A junior college that I said I would never go to. But, I had to swallow my pride and go there. Not to mention they ran out of scholarships and I had to pay my own way. I even quit a good job as the painter for the Pepsi-Cola Bottling Co. My job was to take the old machines, find the dents in them, bondo them up, sand them and then paint them to look new. That job paid about three hundred and twenty five dollars a week in 1980. I went back to the junior college in 1983. Before going back to junior college I wrote Dean Smith and John Thompson respectively after they had each won their national championship in the early eighties. In the letter that I wrote I stated that I was a young man looking for an opportunity to further my education and that I am better than anybody that you have on your team at this time. I received a letter from both coaches saying that they go through the recruiting process to bring in players. Heartbroken, I ripped those letters up. Mind you I didn't write Fairleigh Dickinson or

Pepperdine University, I wrote the national champions. That's how good I knew I was. In 1983 I'm 20 years old now going on 21. My clock is ticking concerning the NBA. The year before that coach Bill Hodges, who was Larry Birds college coach was the coach at the junior college. My brother begged me to go back that year. We had just moved in a small efficiency type apartment. One bed, a couch, a stove, a refrigerator, a bathroom and a T.V. Not to mention I had just got him a job working at the Pepsi-Cola Bottling Company where he still works today may I add. He was telling me he would foot the bill and not to worry about anything but, I knew what they was paying him wasn't going to be able to pay the rent. He knew and I did to that Coach Hodges would recognize my talent and maybe take me with him to his next major college destination. In 1983, coach Hodges was gone and in comes one of the most racist men living. This coach came in from Texas. He would curse players, he kicked a player, and he told racist jokes, just somebody who should have never been in the coaching profession. I was still doing my thing with the marijuana, drinking and cocaine. I played well but, the coach would only play me when we were away from our home court. I knew something was wrong but I couldn't put my hands on what was the problem. I'm the best player on the team, the leader on the team and I should be because I was older, but I'm always on the bench. One home game the racist coach couldn't take it anymore. He let the cat out of the bag. He told the starting point guard, who was black, that he was tired of playing him because of his father. The point guard's father was a legendary coach in our area. He was trying to please this man by playing his son. This man's son couldn't carry my sneakers for me let alone out play me, but he was starting over me. The point guard got up, changed out of his uniform and went and set in the stands with his family. I was happy as can be. I was thinking national junior college championship. The first eight points we scored I was involved with. Four points and two assist. In between coming up the court after scoring the points and handing out the assists, I could see the point guard's father's face. Throughout that game I knew the point guard would be back. Our next game the point guard was in the starting lineup. No more national junior college championship. This went on the rest of the season. The next year the coach took my scholarship and gave it to a player from New York. We had multiple players from New York on the team. These players took the scholarship money and left. I ended up paying my way again. When these players left the coach gave me my scholarship back. The coach displayed some of the worse behavior that could have been displayed for someone who called himself a coach. We would later boycott practice which I organized. During the break from classes I rounded up all the players that were significant in us winning and I told them if anybody goes to practice today they were going to have to fight me. The foolish antics of the coach had gone too far. He wasn't giving us our proper allotment when we went to tournaments. He made us share two for one breakfasts. Like I couldn't eat four pancakes and four sausages. The straw that broke the camel's back was when we were four hours away from home and because we lost a game he said he wasn't stopping for us to eat. Well he did stop for gas and I left the back of the van to go and open the door. The coach asks me what was I doing and I said I'm going to get me something to eat. He got upset but it was nothing he could do. When I got home I called one of the local newspaper reporters that did our games and told him of all the antics. He got in touch with other players and got their side of how the coach conducted business and the story was printed the next day. Then the boycott happened. When it was time for practice there were only three players in the gym and they were walk ons. That afternoon we had another coach. Again, I'm writing this so that you will have a better incite of the man with the perspective. My basketball journey ended in 1985 after two years in junior college. I left needing four credits for an associate of arts degree in Journalism and Communication. In 2000 I did go back and get those four credits to prove to Jaevery if you wanted something bad enough you could achieve it. Jaevery was twelve years old at the time and I wanted to do something impressionable. I not only got the four credits but, I made an A or a B in the classes I took. I had the option to have my degree mailed to me or I could walk with the graduating class. I chose to walk with the graduating class so that Jaevery could picture himself doing it. After that commencement was over I gave Jaevery the degree holder and told him now it's your turn. I was three years sober during the time I went back to school. I quit smoking marijuana in 1988. I don't remember the exact date but it was around Christmas of 1988. I had smoked a joint and later as I was driving I was driving in the wrong lane heading toward oncoming traffic. I righted myself, drove home and never smoke marijuana again. I quit cold turkey. You couldn't pay me to smoke again. I remember thinking this stuff is different. This is not the same marijuana that took a whole bag to get you high. One joint had me and two of my friends out of there. That did it for me concerning marijuana. Cocaine and drinking went on for another nine years ending in 1997. I was a functional user. I was able to go to work and do my job on a high level. I only did the snorting and drinking on the weekends or if I was off work. I tried to stop many time and would for about a month then something would always drag me back to it. This happened about five or six times. Then it happened. The dealer I used to buy from, who was a good friend of mine, would give me cocaine knowing I was getting paid that week or I would show him my check verifying that I got paid that week. I had my check ready and I called him up. When he arrived I couldn't find that check for nothing in the world. I tore my living room up looking for that check. I flipped couches and everything trying to find that check. Finally, my partner said,"Mac when you find the check call me." He wasn't going to give me anything until he knew I could pay. That's just how he rolled. It was about 5:45a.m. The day was October 25, 1997 I will never forget that day. I went down on my knees and I cried out to Jesus telling him that I didn't want to do this anymore, please take the drinking and the desire for cocaine away from me. I was slobbering, hollering and snotting for at least thirty to thirty five minutes. When I got up off my knees I felt brand new. The desire to drink or snort cocaine was gone. You talk about what the power of Jesus can do. I know who I was in that arena of drugs and alcohol, but Jesus set me free from that. I loved Hennessey straight and any kind of beer you could drink. Snorting cocaine was my get away. To not have a thought to indulge again is nothing but Jesus. That was what I did for almost seventeen years. God told his angels to go and take care of that young man he is ready now he will never go back, Holy Spirit touch him! At the same time my ten year old son asked me if he could play recreation football. He said to me "when I'm over my cousin's house I hit boys that are bigger than me and I bring them down". I had to apologize to Jaevery for exposing alcohol to him when he opened the refrigerator for milk, soda, water or some orange juice. I told him that I should have never had beer or liquor next to the drinks that he drank. I told him for the rest of my life he will never see me drink alcohol again. As I write this I'm going on eighteen years of sobriety and it feels marvelous. What was I thinking putting a substance up my nose and poison in my system? The hurt of not being the one to feed my family was an overwhelming burden that only the love of Jesus could feel. I was always a good person from my childhood to this present day, everybody liked me. I was a captain on every team I was on. Even the junior college team players looked up to me although I didn't start they knew I was the man. During my stent with drugs I never hurt anyone other than not being as effective as I could have been to my immediate family. What I'm talking about here is the money I spent and the time I spent hanging out with the fellas getting high. The man behind the perspective is real. What I wanted to happen in my life I made sure that it happen for Jaevery. My dad never once played catch with me or coached my little league teams. My dad only saw me play one game in high school. It was a basketball game against Pahokee High School the season of my junior year. I had twenty two points, eight assists, five steals, seven rebounds and a nice dunk. I remember it this way because my dad was there. It was early in the game and I was at the free throw line and I saw him walk in. I always felt unstoppable, after I saw my dad, I was. The presence of my dad made a difference. I felt that inside of me. For that reason alone I vowed that if I had a son and he was involved in athletics, I would always be there for him. Also people in authority treat your son or daughter better when the father is present. This book is about my perspective on what I witnessed during Jaevery's tenure at that University in the Midwest. I felt a lot of things could have been done better and I expressed that in this book. Just think what would have happened if I was never there? I was able to give my son a life time full of memories that we still talk about today. My dad's ineptitude turned out to be my aptitude. Jaevery often talks about how he felt when he looked up in the stands and I was the only dad in those stands. My dad was a good man and a good provider for our family, but he just wasn't hands on in the area of sports or academics. The only time he was hands on was when he was actually putting hands on, if you know what I mean. When I say that Jaevery slept in the house with a champion, I'm talking about what was given to me after I got up off my knees on October 25, 1997. I was a better husband, father, son, brother, friend and man. I was equipped to do the job that I would face when Jaevery left for that Midwest City. Jesus gave me calmness, a peace and an ability to handle any situation with a what would Jesus do mentality. Peace stayed with me. Peace was in my home, in my car and on my job. I was called the nicest man on my job. There were co-workers that called me a saint because of the way I handle myself. I'm not saying that I was all that, but what was in me made me try hard to be all that.

This book comes from the bottom of my heart. I was blessed to watch Jaevery at five fall camps and four spring practice sessions for a total of ninety three days. What I saw and heard during that time shaped my perspective on how coaches go about their business. Believe me the coaches look at what they do as a business. From my perspective, to do it well you have to implement curtain principles. The structure of a football program is similar to that of a business. There is a mission statement, policy, and procedures and there is an overall expectation of each individual. If there is no expectation there should be. The approach and delivery to those that you supervise or lead is essential to the overall success of the program. The way you talk to people has a definite effect on the performance of the individual. People don't care how much you know until they know how much you care. It's funny how coaches can come in the homes of young men and be the politest person you've ever met, but when they are on the field they turn into these egotistical jerks, who think that profanity laced comments and statements are needed to motivate eighteen to twenty three years old young men. I beg to differ that you can attract more bees with honey than you can with vinegar. The ability to communicate effectively is a trait that all coaches don't have. Coaches lose players every season due to their inability to relate to players and their issues. Coaches don't have time to be a pastor, psychologist, professor, psychiatrist, friend and they definitely don't have time to be daddy or a father figure. Young coaches today like the head coach and defensive coordinator that Jaevery played for are definitely not the father figure type. They're the type of coaches that hope you go through your four or five years at the university problem free. They would rather not deal with problems. But, problems show your overall ability to handle the position as a coach. Mistakes make you a better person. The way your leader handle you during the time of a mistake helps the growth of the person. Life skills should also be taught during troubled times. Parent's it's a crap shoot with these coaches. You roll the dice and pray to God that the coach that recruits your son or daughter have his or her best interest at heart. Not only do promises get broken, but hearts do too. Your sons and daughters are going away sometimes for the first time. They are going to have to adapt to different surroundings and have to follow different rules and regulations. The face of the university will always win over your son or daughter. Ask S. C., A. P. and the pass rush extraordinaire. Your son and daughter are not under your discipline anymore. The things that you would use as teaching tools when he or she made a mistake will now be ruled with an iron hand. It is very imperative that you parents or guardians understand that there will be mini storms and fires that the coaches aren't going to waste their time trying to calm or put out. You the parents or guardians are going to have to be equipped to do so. Keeping your son or daughter encourage is the key to him or her continuing to move forward if he or she is ever under duress. The enemy (devil) would like for you and your son or daughter to spend time worrying about the circumstance, problems, issues, incidents, and situations. But, when you know that no weapon that is formed against you shall be able to prosper, you stay encourage with strong faith knowing that you are going to win. What you as a parent or guardian envision for your son or daughter can come to pass. I'm a witness to this. If God did it for me, he will do it for you. Speak victory over your son or daughter. The Bible says to call those things that be not as though they were (Romans4:17). Words are not just noises and sounds they are spirits too. God said my words will not return unto me void, they will accomplish that which I please, and it shall prosper in the thing whereto I sent it (Isaiah 55:11).

I mentioned how the coaches run their programs like a business. So does the athletic director, the president of the university and every other entity that have anything to do with college football. Money is the number one focus in the world of college football, but the product, which is the players are not paid. It is said that the tradeoff is the full scholarship that a player receive. That is quite the contrary. I wish I would have met a booster or any individual that could have helped me circumvent some of the cost when I made trips to that Midwest City. With all due respect, I would have taken the money. I think the parents of a player should have money for plane flights, hotel fees, car rentals and food reimbursement. My wife and I still bought groceries, clothing and had to give Jaevery money just to have if he saw something he liked or if an emergency came up. I went through a 401k, annual and sick leave and also money that I had in another account. Books, tuition and a place to stay is a beautiful thing, don't get me wrong I can't knock that. But, how much money was made by the football program while Jaevery played? Five bowl appearances at let's say three to four million dollars a bowl game. You're talking between fifteen to twenty million dollars or maybe more and the player can't be paid anything. That money goes where? One might say it helps to support the other sports, it pays salaries for coaches or it does a multi-facet of things concerning the overall athletic department. All these things are probably true. So what that shows me is the structure to pay the players is there. Consider the football players as employees. The only reason they are considered amateurs is because they are not being paid. Every young man on a football team is old enough to work at any job in America. You mean to tell me because their books, tuition and room and board is free they can't make a salary from the university. They can if you change the rules. These rules have been in place for many years and need to be revisited. The financial infrastructure of college football has drastically changed. There is too much money being made to not have the players be compensated for their play. In business the objective is to make a profit. You can't tell me that these major universities are not making a profit each year. The scholarship money that is used for books, tuition, room and board has been sitting in some bank collecting interest for the last twenty or twenty-five years or more. The NCAA and each university can give out scholarships the next hundred years based on the system that they use today. What do the universities have in place? Let me see, the structure to teach is there by having the professors and such, the playing field is there to play. Now all we need is the players and we have that too. What is a scholarship or a letter of intent? They are just pieces of paper. Change the date each year and the name, how easy is that? The system is set up to bring in players for the next three hundred years. The NCAA has a system that has to be revamped. The money that players receive when they do receive money from the university goes to pay for rent, utilities and other necessities. You sure couldn't save anything. Paying players a salary will never cut into the capital that the NCAA and universities make a year or have already made. Throughout the football season the university brings in revenue from parking, advertising, marketing, vending, tickets sales, television and other venues. At the season's end the one game season starts that is ran by the NCAA called the bowl season. The NCAA sale these games to sponsors and big businesses. This is done at the risk of whom, the players. How many coaches, athletic directors or university presidents get hurt in bowl games? How many NCAA executives get hurt for that matter? Not only does the NCAA get paid, but also both teams. Here again, money coming into the university and the players not benefiting. Coaches are paid bonuses when their team makes it to a bowl game. They negotiate their contracts with bowl game incentive bonuses. The coaches are aware of every monetary profit that is made by the football team and they don't miss a beat trying to get that money in their contract. But, the players can't get paid! How can a head coach go from making one million dollars a year to let's say three million dollars a year? The answer is always the players. It's not about the x's and the o's, it's about the Jimmy and Joes. There are little intricacies that you can get better at as a coach. But, the head coach's pay raise come from the play of his players. Why not increase the worth of the scholarships and allow the difference in the money to be given to the players whenever head coaches receive a raise. The head coach or his coaches don't play one down of football, but what they do is deemed worthy of monetary increase when the young men they oversee perform well. The athletic directors and the presidents also have their hands in the money. I'm not knocking the coaches getting paid or anyone getting paid that's in the football program, but how can you leave out the product, which is the players. The salaries that the coaches get all the way down to the equipment managers were a process that was thought out. Somebody signed off and said okay; yes we are going to pay you that amount of money. But, how could they not include the people that are the most at risk. Billions of dollars are being made off the blood, sweat, tears and many times broken bones of these players. The scars and injuries they sustain are sometimes everlasting. Although the players receive proper care at the time of their injuries, some of these injuries linger and is life changing. After the players leave the university the insurance stop. There should be money allocated so that a player can rehabilitate until he has recovered fully. Jaevery told me about how J. C.'s mother paid to have his knee operated on after his senior season was over. J. C. got hurt the last game of the season and didn't play in the bowl game. He should have been still been under the university's medical staff's care. There was a lot of differences between the two parties, thus that young man's mother ended up paying for his knee surgery. This is just an example of why something needs to be in place. Indifferences between a player shouldn't cost a mother thousands of dollars. Again, this is coming from a father's perspective.

  I've been watching college football since the early seventies. I didn't know about the word exploitation at the age of nine or ten, but as I grew older it became familiar to me. The word exploitation can be defined by two words and they are college football. There are too many different entities in college football that's making money to not have the players be paid. To stop the disenfranchisement and financial rape that the NCAA is administering to these young men, I propose that Nike, Adidas, Reebok, Under Armor, Converse and any other major business conglomerate build their own football academy. They could solicit some of the top professors in the country and abroad to work for them. Then you get the same five, four and some three star recruits to come and play for these academies. Pay these young men nice reasonable salaries and watch the NCAA scramble to compete with this market. The television deal will be an automatic attraction because of the top flight high school players and their previous coverage on ESPN. What kid wouldn't want to wear whatever sports gear's company apparel every day. The other businesses can create their own special package to entice the young man to choose their academy. It can be something like paying off the family mortgage, paying off a car note or two, taking care of little brother or little sister's braces. You might say this sound outrageous, but it's the same thing that signing bonuses and shoe contracts allow you to do. You have the right to come up with your own package. Isn't that what the NCAA did and is still doing. They are saying if you want to continue playing football after high school will give you and education, pay for it, give you a place to stay and feed you for four to five years. Their enticement package is the best because there is no competition. I'm just proposing some competition here. What kid wouldn't want to play for the Academy of Mercedes Benz or the JPMorgan Chase Academy? I suffice to say not only would the top high school players come and play but, other players would transfer away from major universities to play for pay at these academies. Whatever it is that allows a high school kid to come out of high school and play one A, double A and triple A baseball and make millions of dollars, the same bylaws should be put into place to govern these academies. You tell me, what is the difference? You are right, there is none. The NCAA has a monopoly on college football and they need to be challenge in a civil suit in antitrust court. Antitrust laws are there to encourage market competition, businesses to compete fairly and to prevent monopolies. What the NCAA is doing seems to fit this definition. Again, this is coming from a father's perspective. Play for pay in college football should be common place by now. Why do you think the number of division one teams has risen? The answer is that the division two universities see how much revenue is being generated by the division one universities and they do what is necessary to reach the division one level. There are one hundred and twenty division one universities that play football under the NCAA. That's billions of dollars that is circulating in that market. Why not expand it with these proposed academies. It is what the NCAA did when the BCS was created. The NCAA took its four best bowls and sold them to create more revenue for whom? Answer, you already know, the NCAA. The Rose Bowl, Orange Bowl, Sugar Bowl and the Fiesta Bowl have always been significant bowls, but the NCAA made them more significant by adding the BCS to it. What is the BCS? I know it stood for Bowl Championship Series, but it was created to make more money for specific men and women. Quite frankly, who is the NCAA? We get caught up in these letters and forget that there are men and now women that are making millions to billions of dollars off the backs of eighteen to twenty three year olds. It's a good business, but bad practices that's been going on way to long. This major cooperation has been getting away with this for too long. I'm just a father with a perspective on this, but there are others out there with the financial muscle to fight the NCAA on this and win. There is a market that can be created where players can be paid and the business owner can make a substantial profit. Some of the sports apparel companies that I mentioned already sponsor the best seven on seven football tournaments in the country. These events are on major television stations and the best high school players in the country are featured. The foundation to start is there, now the structure is needed. I have the vision, but I lack the provision. This product will feed the NFL for the next hundred years or more. Again, nothing against the NCAA, but let's be fair here.

A 130,000 dollar scholarship for a fifth year senior comes to 26,000 dollars a year. That's approximately five hundred and twenty three dollars a week, which come to approximately one thousand and ninety two dollars a month. If you take out the week for spring break, the three weeks for winter break, the week for thanksgiving, and the end of the year time off, you are talking about being off for close to nine weeks. That's approximately forty-five hundred dollars that is not accounted for and the 26,000 dollars is now 21,500 dollars a year. Let's call the early morning weightlifting, going to class, going to meetings, going to practices and then meetings after practices work. Ten hour work days would be the equivalent to four dollars and fifty five cents an hour. Eight hour work days would be the equivalent to five dollars and sixty eight cents an hour. Six hour work days would be the equivalent to seven dollars and fifty eight cents an hour. Four hour work days would be the equivalent to eleven dollars and thirty seven cents an hour. Everybody knows that these young men spend way more than four hours a day being involved in their football related activities. During fall camp these young men are at the football facility for approximately fifteen to sixteen hours and sometimes more. Anywhere else in America you are paid overtime after eight hours of work. Where is the justice here? If you look at what these young men do as a job, they are being grossly under paid. For what these young men do and the money that is generated from their talents, their pay should be enough to where they have money put away to start life after football. The aforementioned academies is a way to make that happen. Now the NCAA has created another money maker called the Playoffs. This is where the top four teams battle it out to see who will win The National Championship. The number one team plays the number four team and number two and three teams play each other. The winners then play each other for The National Championship. Multiple sponsors and revenue streams comes from this new alignment to achieve a champion. The players are still not in the big picture concerning their worth in what these games gross after all is said and done.

WHERE ARE THEY NOW

Some of the teammates that Jaevery played with went on to play professional football in the NFL. Weak side linebacker J. C. went on to win two Super Bowls while playing with the New Orleans Saints and the New England Patriots. He is now playing for his home state of New Jersey with the New York Giants. The Giants play all their home games in East Rutherford, New Jersey. Strong side linebacker D. L. is in his seventh season for the Detroit Lions and has been outstanding there. Defensive end O' B. S. has played in two Super Bowls with the Seattle Seahawks. Tight end G. G. has been with the Houston Texans going into his sixth season. Jaevery's roommate is now married and staying in his hometown of Ft. Lauderdale, Fl. They just had a beautiful daughter name Emory. Jaevery was the best man in the wedding. My wife and I also attended. The head coach is now coaching in the south recruiting and coaching the same type of kids that he didn't want to express themselves when they were in the Midwest. All of a sudden these types of kids are okay to be around and coach here in the south because he needs that type of disposition to win in the south. The defensive coordinator is in the south also coaching. Coincidence, I think not. Both of these coaches have been recruiting in the south for years. They know that to win at the highest level you have to talent. Most of the skilled talent that is needed to win is in the south. But, while these same two coaches were in the Midwest they made the young men they recruited from the south suppress their personalities. I saw the defensive coordinator in the middle of the locker room dancing with his new players. It looked so hypocritical, but I understood what he was doing. He was adapting to his environment just like the head coach was doing the same thing. When the head coach left his first major college coaching job he didn't have the common curtsey to even let the man that hand pick him over other qualified candidates know that he was taken the job down south, he just up and left. Coaches preach honesty and morality but when it come to them they make a way to escape doing or being that. This book is about my perspective of what I witnessed while my son was playing major college football for five years. These two coaches were the focal point of my son's everyday life while there for those five years. My son was able to deal with their insults, politics, reasoning, rationalization along with all the other adversities that he had to face because THE GOOD LORD allowed HIS HOLY SPIRIT to lead me in directing my son through the maze of ups and downs of being a student athlete. The head coach didn't have any kids at the time Jaevery was at that Midwest University and I think the defensive coordinator had two sons during that time. I know they have dealt with multiple young men since they have dealt with Jaevery. But, I would think if their son or sons would be placed in the situations that they placed Jaevery in, that they would be proud if their son or sons would handle themselves like Jaevery handled himself when he was with them.

www.ingramcontent.com/pod-product-compliance
Lightning Source LLC
Chambersburg PA
CBHW071506070526
44578CB00001B/455